Where Your Treasure Is
7 Christian Plays for Youth

AMY L. LAURENS

OTHER WORKS
Find other works by the author at
http://www.amylaurens.com/books/

Where Your Treasure Is

7 Christian Plays for Youth

AMY L. LAURENS

Inkprint PRESS

www.inkprintpress.com

Copyright © 2014 Amy Laurens

2 4 6 8 10 9 7 5 3

In purchasing this book, you have purchased the LIMITED RIGHT to make ONE SCRIPT COPY PER ACTOR, PLUS ONE DIRECTORIAL COPY. Further copying of scripts constitutes a breach of copyright.

All rights reserved. Apart from as listed above, no part of this book may be reproduced in any form or by any electronic or mechanical means, including information storage and retrieval systems, without permission in writing from the publisher, except by a reviewer, who may quote brief passages in a review.

This is a work of fiction. All characters, organisations and events are the author's creation, or are used fictitiously.

ISBN-13
978-1-925825-91-6

www.inkprintpress.com

Library of Congress Cataloguing-in-Publication Data
Laurens, Amy 1985 –
Where Your Treasure Is
234 p.
ISBN-13
 978-1-925825-91-6
Inkprint Press, Newcastle, Australia
    1. Christian Drama 2. Bible—Drama 3. Children's Plays 4. Bible Plays

First Edition
August 2014

Printed in the United States of America.

Cover design © Amy Laurens.

COPYRIGHT NOTICE

In purchasing this book, you have purchased the LIMITED RIGHT to make ONE SCRIPT COPY PER ACTOR, PLUS ONE DIRECTORIAL COPY. Further copying of scripts constitutes a breach of copyright.

All rights reserved. Apart from as listed above, no part of this book may be reproduced in any form or by any electronic or mechanical means, including information storage and retrieval systems, without permission in writing from the publisher, except by a reviewer, who may quote brief passages in a review.

CONTENTS

1   Drive

2   Where Your Treasure Is

3   The 5000

4   Gifts

5   Turning Point

6   In Search of Freedom

7   The Journey

DRIVE

In *Drive*, two separate storylines merge as two young people learn what it really means to be in control of your own life. Naomi, prompted by her mother Karen and her friend Alex, takes the important step of getting back behind the wheel a year after a horrible accident that left her then-boyfriend dead; Jason, spurred on by his friend Chad, makes plans to steal the car he's been lusting after all year.

However, when Jason and Chad agree to repay the favour to the woman who organised the car heist, things go horribly wrong: a simple store-theft becomes an armed hold-up with hostages. One of the hostages, Naomi finds herself challenged to apply everything her mother and friend have been telling her about trusting herself, and with some quick thinking she sets out to diffuse the situation.

The police arrive and arrest the thieves. Back at the police station, Naomi figures out what it really means to be in the driver's seat, and Jason is crushed as he learns that his father had planning to buy the car he's stolen for his birthday. In the end, he learns that sometimes, being in control of your own life still means choosing to trust and wait on others.

ACTORS REQUIRED

Male
3

Female
6*

Either
2, plus extras.

MINIMUM TOTAL
8 plus extras.

* KAITLAN is scripted as female, but could be changed to male.

NOTE: The type of car is deliberately left blank for the director to fill in as appropriate.

DRIVE

SCENE SUMMARIES

ACT I

SCENE 1
Jason's father leaves for work and Jason, despondent over his father's brush-off, leaves for a friend's house.

SCENE 2
Alex confronts Naomi about the car accident that haunts her, and Naomi decides to take Alex's advice and try driving again.

SCENE 3
Chad convinces Jason to see a girl about stealing the car he's longing for.

ACT II

SCENE 1
Naomi bravely attempts to drive, and someone crashes into her.

SCENE 2
Chad and Jason meet Gwen, the girl who will help them steal the car.

ACT III

SCENE 1
Naomi is confronted by both her mother and Alex, who insist that she can't just give up on life, God, and everything. People are looking up to her, watching her—and she has a responsibility to set an example for them.

DRIVE

ACT IV

SCENE 1
Jason and Chad meet up with Gwen once more, and prepare to steal the car.

SCENE 2
The car is stolen.

ACT V

SCENE 1
Naomi appears to conquer her fear, and drives herself and Alex to the supermarket.

SCENE 2
In the supermarket, Naomi muses about what gave her the courage to drive.

SCENE 3
Chad and Gwen rob a supermarket, but with Jason's help it all goes wrong.

ACT VI

SCENE 1
Now a potential hostage, Naomi has to overcome her fears and calm the other girls down.

ACT VII

SCENE 1
The girls try to escape. Gwen spots them, and the negotiations begin...

ACT VIII

SCENE 1
Naomi discusses with Alex and then with Karen the nature of trust, and being trusted.

SCENE 2
Jason comes face to face with his father, and finally gets his orange.

DRIVE

CAST OF CHARACTERS

FATHER
A respected businessman in his late forties. Kind and wise, loving – but busy.

JASON
In his late teens, filled with uncertainty about himself and his value in his father's eyes.

ALEX
Naomi's best friend—a practical, sensible girl who thinks there's never any real reason to get emotional.

NAOMI
A sweet and mild-mannered girl who lacks confidence in her abilities and self.

CHAD
Boy in his late teens who's been mixing with the wrong crowd. Has utter faith in his ability to look after himself.

GIRL
An extra. Fashionable, attractive, and trendy.

GWEN
A thief. Attractive, sensible, intelligent.

KAREN
Naomi's mother. In her late thirties. Caring, wise, loving and with a knack for odd metaphors.

SHOPKEEPER
An extra. Onstage for acts 6 and 7; no lines.

KAITLAN
A young girl, about 12, caught in the hostage situation.

POLICEMAN 1
An extra. Two or three other policemen also required.

DRIVE

ACT I

Scene 1

JASON sits slumped at a kitchen table. There is a BOWL OF ORANGES and a MOBILE PHONE on the table. Behind him is a WINDOW.

                    FATHER (O.S.)

Jason! I'm leaving now. I want that mess in the lounge room tidied up before tonight please.

                    JASON

Whatever.

                    FATHER

Not whatever. It's been out for a week. I want it gone. (*beat*) I'm going. Bye!

                    JASON

Come here?

                    FATHER

I'm late, Jason.

                    JASON

But I'm hungry.

                    FATHER

There's a bowl full of fruit on the table.

                    JASON

I know, but... (*beat*) Oh, never mind. (*Picks up an ORANGE*).

                    FATHER

I'm late! Goodbye!

A door closes. JASON moves to the window and looks outside. A car starts.

JASON

Of course you're late. You're always late.

JASON contemplates the ORANGE, then throws it across the stage. JASON flops onto chair again. The MOBILE PHONE rings.

JASON

Hello? Yeah, sure, I'll come over. Meet you on the corner? Yeah, okay, see you in ten. Bye.

JASON hangs up the PHONE and exits.

Scene 2

NAOMI and ALEX loll around in the lounge room of NAOMI'S house. A KEY RACK with CAR KEYS hangs on a wall.

ALEX

I'm bored.

NAOMI

What do you want to do?

ALEX

I don't know. Something fun.

NAOMI

DVD?

ALEX shakes her head.

NAOMI

Board game?

ALEX

Let's go out.

NAOMI

Out where?

DRIVE

ALEX
Shops?

NAOMI
But that's too far to walk in this heat...

ALEX
(*rolls eyes*) I know. That's why we drive.

NAOMI
No way. You know I can't.

ALEX
Can't? It's got nothing to do with can't. "Won't" is the word you're looking for, I think.

NAOMI
Alex, it's not like that. You know that.

ALEX
Nome, it's been three months. You can't hold onto it forever. You're going to have to get over it sooner or later.

NAOMI
I'd rather later, thanks.

ALEX
Later when? When you're too old to drive anyway?

NAOMI
(*mumbling*) Sounds good to me.

ALEX
Nome, you can't let the accident ruin your life. So you had a crash, big deal. It was one moment in time. Don't make it the rest of your life.

NAOMI
A crash? You think this is just about having a *crash*? He died, Alex! Jesse *died*! I killed him!

ALEX
Naomi, we've been through this a hundred times. It's not your fault. His parents don't blame you, your parents don't blame you, the police don't, I don't, no one does except you. Don't you think you need to cut yourself a little slack?

NAOMI

Why should I, Alex?

ALEX

Maybe so /you can have a *life*...

NAOMI

Because he certainly didn't get any slack, did he? He's *dead*, he doesn't *get* slack. No second chances, no do-overs, no opportunity to start again and "get over it".

ALEX

Naomi...

NAOMI

Don't, Alex. I've heard it all before.

ALEX

(*angry*) Well maybe you have. So what? It's clearly not getting through to you, so it bears repeating.

NAOMI

Just shut /up.

ALEX

No, you shut up. Listen to me. And I mean actually listen, like with your brain, not just your ears. You wasting the rest of your life isn't going to bring him back. It isn't going to justify his death, or make it worthwhile, or meaningful. It isn't going to absolve you of guilt, and it isn't going to fix anything. (*beat*) I'm going to the shops. You can drive, and come with me, or the next time you see me will probably be in hospital where I'll be getting treatment for the infected blisters and heat stroke I'll get from walking all the way there. But I am going. Your life? (*Shrugs.*) That's up to you.

ALEX exits.

NAOMI watches after her. She gets up and crosses to the KEY RACK. She reaches for the KEYS, and hesitates. She snatches up the KEYS, and exits.

Scene 3

CHAD loiters on a street corner, waiting.

Enter JASON.

DRIVE

                              CHAD
Hey.

                              JASON
Hey.

                              CHAD
So, what's up?

                              JASON
Nothing. Dad's just being a jerk again.

                              CHAD
Heh. What's he on your case for this time?

                              JASON
Stuff in the lounge. Wants me to pack up the Xbox, but it's right in the middle of a huge download.

                              CHAD
Bummer.

                              JASON
Yeah.

                              JASON
So. What are we going to do?

                              CHAD
Dunno. (*beat*) Hey, let's go look at your car.

                              JASON
My car?

                              CHAD
Yeah, you know, that (car model) you've been drooling over.

                              JASON
's not *my* car.

                              CHAD
(*grins*) But it will be.

THEY begin walking across stage.

JASON
Psh. Doubtful. I'm never going to be able to afford it.

CHAD
So ask your old man for a loan.

JASON
You kidding me? I'm not asking him.

CHAD
Oh, come on. He can afford it.

JASON
I don't care. I'm not asking him. For anything. Ever. I don't need him.

CHAD
(*shrugs*) Well, whatever.

THEY arrive at the CAR and fawn over it.

GIRL enters.

GIRL
Hey. Nice car.

JASON
You like it? I'm thinking of buying it.

GIRL
(*appraises him*) Take me for a ride when you do.

GIRL winks and exits.

CHAD
(*low whistle*) Hot *dawg*, Jace. You have *got* to get yourself this car!

JASON
I can't afford it!

CHAD
(*thoughtful*) Well, no one said anything about affording it. Other than you, that is.

DRIVE

                    JASON
What are you talking about?

                    CHAD
There are... other options.

                    JASON
Options?

                    CHAD
(*hesitates*) I know someone. Someone who... acquisitions things.

                    JASON
Acquisitions? You mean steals.

                    CHAD
(*shrugs*) Sure, if you want to phrase it so crudely.

                    JASON
(*dubious*) I dunno, Chad. I don't think...

                    CHAD
Don't think what?

                    JASON
I don't think Dad'd like it.

                    CHAD
(*exasperated*) Jace, you've been drooling over this car for *months*. He knows you want it, right?

                    JASON
Well, yeah...

                    CHAD
And he hasn't said anything, has he? Hasn't done anything about it?

                    JASON
No...

                    CHAD
And you're the one who just said you didn't need him. You don't, do you?

                        JASON
No!

                        CHAD
So are you going to look after yourself or not?

                        JASON
All right! All right. Who's this guy you know?

                        CHAD
Well, I met her a couple of years ago, through a mutual friend...

                        JASON
Whoa, whoa whoa. Hold on just one second. *Her?*

                        CHAD
Oh, yeah, didn't I say that? She's a chick.

                        JASON
A chick?

                        CHAD
That's what I said, isn't it? Look, does it really matter? She's good, that's the point. You want something, she gets it.

                        JASON
A chick?

                        CHAD
Get over it already. Do you want to meet her or not?

                        JASON
(*grins*) Is she hot?

                        CHAD
Ah ha, you're funny. Yes or no?

                        JASON
I... Sure. Why not? One meeting can't hurt, right?

                        CHAD
Right.

DRIVE

ACT II

Scene 1

NAOMI and ALEX sit in the front seat of a CAR.

          NAOMI
(*elated*) I can't believe I'm actually doing this!

          ALEX
I can't either.

          NAOMI
This is... this is... Scary.

The CAR slows.

          ALEX
Naomi, it's fine. You're doing well.

          NAOMI
(*tense*) You think so?

          ALEX
Sure! You're doing great!

          NAOMI
(*beat*) Okay.

THEY continue driving in silence.

The CAR turns.

          ALEX
Nearly there. You're doing so well, Naomi!

          NAOMI
Thanks. I—

Tyres screech. ANOTHER CAR collides with NAOMI'S CAR.

NAOMI screams.

          ALEX
What the?

The CAR jerks to a halt.

ALEX
Naomi, are you okay?

NAOMI flings open the CAR DOOR and jumps out.

NAOMI
(*to other driver*) Are you *right* there? I mean seriously, I was just driving here, so don't mind me. It's not like I'm getting over a serious, life-changing accident or anything, and trying to get my life back together. So, you know, just go ahead and *drive into me*. No problem.

ALEX
(*takes NAOMI by the arm*) Nome, c'mon, leave her alone. Let's just wait over here, okay?

THEY sit.

ALEX
Did someone call the police?

NAOMI
I doubt it. If she can't even manage to turn across an intersection without crashing into someone, I doubt she's intelligent enough to think of calling the police.

ALEX
Nome, be nice. (*She pulls out her mobile and dials*). Hello? Yes, I'd like to report a car accident, please...

NAOMI shivers.

Scene 2

CHAD and JASON on a street corner. CHAD hangs up his MOBILE PHONE.

CHAD
Well, you're in luck.

JASON
I am?

DRIVE

CHAD
Yeah. She's actually free right now.

THEY begin to walk.

JASON
I don't know, Chad. I'm still not sure about this whole idea.

CHAD
Oh, come on. Don't get all wussy on me. You want the car, she can get it for you, it's as simple as that.

Silence.

JASON
Not really, though.

CHAD
What?

JASON
Not really that simple. I mean, it's stealing, it's not exactly morally straightforward, is it?

CHAD
And you care about that since when?

JASON shrugs.

Silence.

JASON
Look, I just don't think my Dad's going to like it, all right?

CHAD
And you care because?

JASON
Well, /it's not

CHAD
An hour ago you were whinging about how he's always on your case, and how much you hate him and his rules and whatever. Now you're telling me you want all that?

JASON
No.

CHAD
Good. (*beat*) I mean, he doesn't even have to know, does he?

JASON
I think he's going to notice when I rock up home with a car, Chad.

CHAD
No duh, frog-brain. But he doesn't have to know how you got it, does he?

JASON
Oh, right, so what do I say? He goes, "Son, that's a nice car you have there", and I go, "Yeah, and it just appeared out of thin air, too. Pretty special, huh?" (*gives CHAD a pointed look*) Somehow, I don't think so.

CHAD
(*shrugs*) We'll think of something.

JASON
(*mutters*) Something that doesn't land me in prison, for preference.

THEY continue walking. GWEN appears ahead of them on the street.

CHAD
Oh good, she's here.

THEY approach GWEN.

CHAD
Hi, Ms Anderson.

GWEN
Chad, I've told you a million times: it's Gwen.

CHAD
(*grin*) How are you, Gwen?

GWEN
Fine. This him?

DRIVE

                                                CHAD

Yeah, this is my buddy Jason. He's, ah, got a bit of a problem.

                                                GWEN

What sort?

                                                CHAD

It's a car. Think you can help?

                                                GWEN

We'll see. It all depends.

                                                JASON

Depends? On what?

                                                GWEN

(*to Chad*) On you, for a start. Are you actually going to go through with this, or are you going to chicken out on me at the last minute again? I need someone who's dependable, someone who's not interested in getting caught.

                                                CHAD

Hey, I did not chicken out! That was a genuine mistake! You know that. I'm not interested in getting caught any more than you are!

                                                GWEN

Indeed. After last time, I imagine you're not.

                                                JASON

Last time? What do you mean, 'last time'? (*to CHAD*) Chad, what does she mean, 'last time'?

                                                CHAD

Relax, man. It's nothing. I just got tangled in a little... incident a while ago while I was working for Gwen here.

                                                JASON

You worked for Gwen? How did I not know about this?

                                                CHAD

Ah, it was ages ago, man. Back when you were all churchy and stuff.

                                                JASON

Oh.

GWEN
Charming as this revelatory conversation is, I'm sure, I'm not here as a relationship counselor. So if you don't mind...

CHAD
Right. Sorry. So, ah, what do you want to know?

GWEN
Everything, obviously. But start with what car exactly we're talking about here, and where it is.

CHAD
It's a (car description).

JASON
It's a (more specific car description).

GWEN
(hiding smile) Right. And where is this (more specific car description)?

JASON
(*excited*) It's down at (placename), just opposite the (otherstore).

GWEN
Hmm, yes. I know the place. (*beat*) All right, leave it with me, I'll see if it can be done. I'll give you a call Monday and let you know. You're prepared to pay our standard way?

CHAD
Sure, no problem.

JASON
Pay? Standard way? What—

CHAD
It's fine. No problem at all. We're good, I swear.

GWEN
(*gives him a long look*) You're lucky I know you, Chad-boy. This here (*nods at JASON*) looks like nothing so much as a raw newbie. He's not going to wreck this, is he?

CHAD
He's fine, Gwen. No problem. He's good at following instructions—aren't you Jace?

DRIVE

JASON
Uh, yeah, sure. I can follow instructions.

GWEN
Good. Well. I'll be in touch.

GWEN exits.

JASON
Instructions? Payment? Chad, what are you getting us into?

CHAD
It's nothing, man, it's all cool. I know her. It's sweet.

JASON
But I can't afford to pay her off! I thought that was the whole point of this—I have no money, so we... appropriate the car.

CHAD
(*grin*) Still can't say it, can you?

JASON
Say what?

CHAD
Stealing, Jason, my man. We're stealing the car.

JASON
Oh, shut up.

CHAD
Look, seriously, it's all fine. She doesn't want money.

JASON
Then what does she want? (*beat*) Surely you don't mean...

CHAD
(*waves him away*) No, man! Geez, settle down. She's not into that. Look, if I know Gwen—and I do—payment just means she'll need help with a little job first, to make sure we're good for it.

JASON
Good for what?

CHAD

Did you leave your brain behind today or something? Good to help her.

JASON

Help her?

CHAD

Are you going to repeat everything I say? Yes, help her. You don't think she's going to nick the car all by her lonesome, now, do you?

JASON

Well, /I

CHAD

Look, it's nothing. Mostly, it's just something like driving the getaway vehicle or something. Nothing too heavy.

JASON

Mostly? Do I want to know how you know that?

CHAD

(*grin*) Probably not.

JASON

(*sighs*) All right. I'll... I'll think about it. I mean, she might come back to us on Monday and say that nothing can be done, anyway. Right?

CHAD

Sure, Jace. You think that if it'll make you happy. And in the mean time, let's go play footy and drool over your car some more.

JASON

It's not my car.

CHAD

Oh, but it will be, Jace. It will be.

THEY exit.

ACT III

Scene 1

NAOMI'S bedroom. She lies on her BED, staring at the ceiling. There is a knock at the DOOR.

DRIVE

                                  KAREN (O.S)

Naomi? Naomi, sweetheart, are you okay?

KAREN pokes her head around the DOOR. NAOMI ignores her.

                                  KAREN

Naomi, honey, please talk to me...

Silence.

                                  KAREN

Well, if you won't talk to me, perhaps you'll talk to Alex.

Enter ALEX.

                                  ALEX

(*quietly*) Hey, Nome.

ALEX crosses to the BED and sits. KAREN watches with concern, then exits. NAOMI continues to ignore ALEX.

                                  ALEX

How are you doing? (beat) Naomi, come on, you have to talk to me.

ALEX flops back onto the bed with NAOMI. Silence.

                                  NAOMI

What's the point?

                                  ALEX

What do you mean?

                                  NAOMI

I mean, what happened happened. You can't change it, I can't change it. So what's the point?

                                  ALEX

The point? The point is for you to be able to find some sort of closure. For you to be able to get over this whole mess, /to get your

                                  NAOMI

Get over it, get over it! That's all anyone can say to me at the moment. Well, what if I don't *want* to "get over it"? What if I'm happy how I am?

ALEX

(*laughs nervously*) Happy? Naomi, I think we can all agree that's the last thing you are right now.

NAOMI

Well, so what? I don't care, so why should anyone else?

ALEX

Because we care about you, you idiot.

Silence.

NAOMI

I killed him, you know.

ALEX

Naomi, I /told you

NAOMI

No. You want me to talk, then shut up and let me talk. It was my fault. I killed him. No, I didn't do it on purpose, and no, I didn't know he would die, or mean for him to, but I still did it. It's still my fault.

ALEX

Naomi, /it's not your

NAOMI

It *is*. It *is* my fault. Nothing anyone says will convince me otherwise, Alex. I was driving, I was in control, it was *my* fault.

ALEX

Well, so what if it is?

NAOMI

What?

ALEX

So what if it is? You can't just give up. You've got to keep living.

NAOMI

Alex, I can't. Don't you think I've heard what everyone's saying about me? What they think of me? Don't you think I see the looks every time I go down to the store, hear the whispers as I walk down the street? Everyone knows, and everyone blames me.

DRIVE

ALEX
So what?

NAOMI
Are you not listening to me? They hate me! Everyone hates me!

ALEX
I'm listening to you. I just think you're wrong.

NAOMI
Alex, /I

ALEX
I know what you think, and I know how you're feeling.

NAOMI
No you /don't!

ALEX
I do! I've heard you talk about it enough over the last three months, I think I know by now, okay? Give me a little credit here! But, and don't bite my head off for this, but here's a thought: Jesse's dead. You're not. (*hesitates, waiting to see if NAOMI will react*). So, I think there's a reason you're still alive.

NAOMI
What?

ALEX
I think there's a reason you're still alive.

NAOMI
(*rolls her eyes*) Alex, don't tell me you're going to start spouting all that God crap /now.

ALEX
Just listen, for a second, will you? I know you think you've decided that there is no God, or if there is then He doesn't care about you, and that the whole situation is His idea of a bad joke or something... But really. Wouldn't you *like* there to be some meaning behind all this?

NAOMI
I... (*sighs*) Yes. No. Maybe. I mean, sure, I do, but isn't that just wishful thinking? Fabricating a meaning for something just to make myself feel better isn't really meaningful, is it?

ALEX
It's not fabricating, Naomi. You have to live, and to live, you have to have something to live for.

NAOMI
And I don't.

ALEX
Only because you won't *let* yourself. You've given up.

NAOMI
Well, so what if I have?

ALEX
So what? So what? What about your sister, Tara? What about all those teens you used to teach at Pathfinders? Naomi, those kids look up to you. They watch what you're doing whether you want them to or not. I know you'd like to think right now that what you do doesn't matter any more, that it would be easier for everyone if you just faded away... But it's not true. You matter to people, Naomi. You matter.

A knock at the DOOR.

KAREN (O.S)
Naomi? Alex?

ALEX
Come in.

KAREN enters.

KAREN
Alex, your mum's here to pick you up.

ALEX
(*to NAOMI*) Okay?

NAOMI nods reluctantly.

ALEX
I love you, girl. It's going to be okay.

ALEX exits.

KAREN
Naomi, sweetie, how are you doing?

DRIVE

NAOMI shrugs.

KAREN
It's okay to feel guilty, you know.

NAOMI looks at her mother in surprise.

KAREN
It's perfectly natural. The ones left behind often question why—why they survived when the other didn't, why they are left to deal with the fallout, why they were somehow preserved when they are clearly the guilty ones.

NAOMI
...You think I'm clearly a guilty one?

KAREN
(*smiles*) That's not what I said.

NAOMI
But you do, though. Everyone does. I am, so why shouldn't they?

KAREN
Naomi... Everyone in life does things they don't intend. Sometimes those things have small consequences – sometimes they have big ones. We can't take back what we've done. We can't choose to erase our mistakes, or reverse our circumstances. But we *can* choose how we react to them.

NAOMI
You want me to be a hero, just like Alex does.

KAREN
No, I want you to pull yourself together, grow up a little, and realise that you're not the only one affected by the accident.

NAOMI
Ouch.

KAREN
(*gently*) Maybe so, but you know it's true.

Silence.

NAOMI
So what, you want me to go out and drive again, just to prove I can? I tried that and it didn't end up too well, or did you miss the massive dents in the side of the Mercedes?

KAREN
Naomi, you don't need to get sarcastic with me, thank you very much. Yes, I want you to start driving again.

NAOMI
Why? So I can demonstrate to the world that good little Naomi, killer of innocent boys, has 'gotten over it' and moved on with her life?

KAREN
(*joking a little*) No, so that you can escape the house, stop being trapped here by your moping. If you want to mope, I can't stop you—but you can at least get out of the house to do it.

NAOMI
The Merc's wrecked, Mum. I couldn't drive it now if I wanted to.

KAREN
We'll get it fixed, sweetie. And in the meantime, I'm borrowing Andrea's car.

NAOMI
I can't drive Andrea's car!

KAREN
Why not?

NAOMI
It's bad enough ruining *your* car. I can't ruin her car as well!

KAREN
You're not going to ruin it, Naomi.

NAOMI
I am, I am going to ruin it! I ruined the Mini, I ruined the Merc, I'm a car ruiner! I'm a murderer and a car wrecker!

KAREN
Naomi, calm down! It was an accident, Naomi, an accident. Definition of an accident not deliberate. You didn't ask for the kangaroo to jump out in front of you, and there was no way to plan for oil on the road. You're not a murderer, and you're not going to wreck Andrea's car.

NAOMI
How do you *know*?

DRIVE

KAREN
I don't. I trust.

NAOMI
Huh. Who? God?

KAREN
Yes, although I know that seems foreign to you right now.

NAOMI
Well, /I

KAREN
(*waves to hush NAOMI*) But I also trust someone I think you'll find much closer to home.

NAOMI
What?

KAREN
I trust you, Naomi.

NAOMI
Thanks, Mum.

KAREN
I trust you, Naomi. I trust you to drive safely, and I trust you to let yourself heal. Your sister looks up to you, you know. If you can't do it for yourself, I know you'll do it for her.

NAOMI
That's what Alex said.

KAREN
Alex is a very wise girl.

ACT IV

Scene 1

JASON and CHAD sit at a TABLE covered with sheets of PAPER – the plans for the heist.

JASON
I still don't know about all of this.

CHAD
Jace, man, you've had a week to consider it. You can't back out now!

JASON
Can too. You just don't want to look like an idiot in front of Gwen.

CHAD
Oh, you're funny. It's nothing to do with that. /It's just

JASON
Oh? Then what was with the flirting yesterday?

CHAD
No idea what you're talking about.

JASON
Oh, come off it. You totally /made a move

GWEN
(*Enters*) Come off what?

CHAD and JASON blush.

JASON
Uh, nothing. Just kidding around.

GWEN
Mm, well, less kidding, more revising, please. We're nearly ready to go.

CHAD
Sure thing, Gwen. We're ready.

GWEN
(*appraises JASON*) I hope so.

CHAD
Oh, don't worry about him! He'll be fine! No problem at all, I promise.

GWEN
(*pointed look at CHAD*) There'd better not be.

GWEN exits.

CHAD flops onto the TABLE with a sigh. JASON raises his eyebrows at him.

JASON

You done yet?

CHAD

Done what?

JASON

Done drooling over her.

CHAD

I was not drooling over her! How could you say that?/ That's

JASON

Yeah, yeah, whatever. I've seen the way you look at her. You're into her, that's fine.

CHAD

(*loudly*) So, about the plan.

JASON

(*rolls eyes*) What about it?

CHAD

I... I don't know. Do you reckon it'll all go okay?

JASON

How am I supposed to know? You're the one who's done this before!

CHAD

I'm not worried about the actual job, so much.

JASON

Then what?

CHAD

(*hesitates*) Don't take this wrong or anything, I trust you, you know that... It's just... I know you're not keen on the whole idea still. How do I know you're not going to bail on us right in the middle of the operation and get us all in trouble?

JASON

Chad, I'm not going to bail on you. Once I'm committed, I'm committed. (*mutters*) Or perhaps committable.

CHAD

Good. Because I'm putting my reputation on the line here for you, you know.

JASON

You have a reputation?

CHAD

I told you. I've been working with Gwen off and on for a few years now.

JASON

Actually, you didn't tell me that.

CHAD

Well I did now.

JASON

Okay, calm down, it's not like I care or anything! I'm just saying, I'm not going to let you down, okay?

CHAD

Honest?

JASON

(*grits teeth*) Yeah, I guess so.

CHAD

(*happy*) Well, you're in for it now then, aren't you!

JASON

You needn't be so overjoyed. You're corrupting me, you know that? Corrupting!

CHAD

Nonsense! I'm setting a good example for you here about what it means to look after yourself. Right?

JASON raises an eyebrow.

CHAD

I mean, look at me. Have you ever seen me bludge off my parents for anything?

JASON

True.

DRIVE

                          CHAD

's right. I'm a man, I take care of myself.

                          JASON

I don't /think

                          CHAD

Look, you agreed to do it, you're not going to bail on me, that's all that matters. Can we stop having the same stupid argument every time?

                          JASON

Fine. So. What's left to do?

Scene 2

JASON, CHAD and GWEN offstage, wearing dark colours, beanies, and dark boot polish on their cheeks.

                          GWEN (O.S.)

Okay, boys, we're nearly there. You ready?

                          CHAD (O.S.)

Sure thing.

                          JASON (O.S.)

Uh huh.

                          GWEN (O.S.)

Right. Let's go.

                          GWEN (O.S.)

Okay, no noise from here on in.

THEY creep slowly across the stage, GWEN in the lead, JASON hanging back a little. JASON bashes his shins into an ITEM OF FURNITURE.

                          JASON

Ouch!

                          GWEN

Shhh!

JASON
(*whisper*) Sorry! I didn't bash my leg on purpose, you know.

GWEN
SHHH!

CHAD
Just shut up, and come on!

JASON hobbles after them, mumbling complaints. At the edge of the stage, GWEN turns back to the BOYS.

GWEN
Okay. Now, I'll go ahead and break the lock. When I signal, Chad, you come and disable the alarm. Bring the equipment with you.

JASON
What should I do?

GWEN
You stay here.

JASON
But—

CHAD
Shh!

GWEN exits. The BOYS fidget while they wait.

JASON
How come you get to go in and help her?

CHAD
I thought you weren't even sure you wanted to be involved.

JASON
Well, I wasn't—I'm not—but if I'm here, I should do something, shouldn't I?

CHAD
Yes. Do something: stay out of the way.

JASON
But it's my car!

DRIVE

CHAD
It won't be if you mess things up for us, or get us caught.

JASON
I'm not going to get us caught!

CHAD
Yeah? So you've got plenty of experience breaking and entering, have you? Know how to pick a lock and disable an alarm system?

JASON
No.

CHAD
Then shut up, and do as you're told.

JASON
It's my car.

CHAD
And do you want it, or not? 'Cause if not, we're wasting our time here, and I'll go tell Gwen right now to call it off... (*makes as though to go find GWEN*)

JASON
All right! All right. I'll stay here. I just hate feeling so useless.

CHAD
Aw, you're not useless. How 'bout you get to be the getaway driver?

JASON
(*grins*) I'd like that.

CHAD
Good, it'll be good practice for later.

JASON
Later?

CHAD
I told you. Gwen helps us, we help her.

JASON
Help with what?

CHAD
(*gives JASON a long look*) How about you find out when we get there?

JASON
(*growing concerned*) How about you tell me now?

GWEN (O.S)
Psst! Chad!

CHAD
Gotta go. Wait here.

JASON
Chad!

CHAD
Wait here!

Breaking glass sounds.

GWEN
Chad!

CHAD
I've got to go!

CHAD exits. An alarm starts, but is quickly shut off. Silence.

JASON starts to pace. An engine starts.

CHAD (O.S. QUIETLY)
Jace! We got it! Come drive!

ACT V

Scene 1

NAOMI and ALEX, in a CAR.

ALEX
So, how are you feeling this time?

NAOMI
Okay, I think.

DRIVE

ALEX
Good.

NAOMI
Good what?

ALEX
What do you mean, 'Good what'?

NAOMI
What did you mean by that tone of voice?

ALEX
Nothing!

NAOMI
Right. I'm sure.

ALEX
Naomi, I just meant it's good that your actually getting out and doing something. Finally.

NAOMI
Finally?

ALEX
Look, it's nothing, it's fine, stop stressing over everything.

NAOMI
I'm not!

ALEX
Then stop reading things into what I'm saying!

NAOMI
I didn't *ask* you to stick around, you know. You could have left at any time.

ALEX
What?

NAOMI
Well, you're obviously sick of me, so why didn't you just leave?

ALEX
Naomi, I know you're stressed about this whole thing, but you're being crazy! I'm glad you're getting out, yes, and yes, it's taken a long time and it got really boring for a while, but you're my friend! I stuck with you because that's what friends do!

Silence.

NAOMI
Really?

ALEX
Of course, you idiot.

NAOMI
(*beat*) Thanks.

ALEX
No problem. (*beat*) We're nearly there. Are you going to be right to park out the back, or do you just want to pull in to the driveway next door?

NAOMI
Next door sounds good.

Indicator sound. The CAR slows, then comes to a halt.

ALEX
Hey, Naomi?

NAOMI
Mm?

ALEX
You made it.

NAOMI
(*grins*) Yeah. I guess I did.

Scene 2

A small SUPERMARKET, empty of customers. Enter NAOMI and ALEX.

NAOMI
I did it! I can't believe I did it!

DRIVE

ALEX
(*grinning*) I can. You did well.

NAOMI
Thanks. So. What are we here for?

ALEX
Your Mum said we need milk and some chocolate.

THEY browse.

ALEX
(*hesitantly*) So, do you think...

NAOMI
What?

ALEX
Never mind.

NAOMI
No, say it. It's okay.

ALEX
Really?

NAOMI
Sure. Go ahead.

ALEX
(*deep breath*) Do you think you're over it now?

NAOMI
I knew it! I knew you were sick of me!

ALEX
I was not sick of you!

NAOMI
Really?

ALEX

I wasn't. It's just... I mean... (*deep breath*) It would be nice to have the old Naomi back again, that's all.

NAOMI

(*beat*) I... I'm not sure.

ALEX

Not sure? Why?

NAOMI

(*shrugs*) I don't think it's the kind of thing you just 'get over', especially not in one go.

ALEX

But?

NAOMI

But... But I guess I'm making a start.

THEY *browse.*

ALEX

So what was it that changed your mind?

NAOMI

What do you mean?

ALEX

What changed your mind? After that girl ran up the back of you last week, I thought that was it, you'd never drive again.

NAOMI

So did I.

ALEX

So what did it, then?

NAOMI

I... I don't know. I guess...

ALEX

Yes?

DRIVE

                              NAOMI
I guess it was what you and Mum said to me, that night you came over.

                              ALEX
Really? I thought you weren't even listening. Which bit?

                              NAOMI
What?

                              ALEX
Which bit? What part of my genius speech inspired you?

                              NAOMI
There's no need to go getting all big-headed about it, you know. Mum spoke to me too.

                              ALEX
Sheesh, way to kill a girl's fun.

                              NAOMI
(*beat*) It was... It was what you both said about having a responsibility, not just to myself, but to everyone else. I... I guess I'd just been lying around, feeling like everyone was looking down on me, like every time I went out they were whispering about me, about how terrible I was, such a failure.

                              ALEX
Nome—

                              NAOMI
But then you said something. About how the younger kids were looking up to me. About how I had to set an example. And I remembered something I heard at church, years ago.

                              ALEX
What?

                              NAOMI
It's a verse, or part of a verse. I can't remember where it's from, or what the rest of it is, but for some reason, this fragment just came to me.

                              ALEX
What is it?

                              NAOMI
"Do not let anyone look down on you because you are young, but set an example."

ALEX
That's it?

NAOMI
No, I told you, there's more, but I don't remember it. But it doesn't matter. That's the important bit. That, and what you said about how I have to live, and reminding me that God has a plan... (*shrugs*) I'm not totally convinced, yet. But I'd like to believe you're right.

ALEX
I said that?

NAOMI
(*rolls eyes*) Yes, Lex.

ALEX
Really? Wow. I'm smarter than I thought.

NAOMI mock punches ALEX, before giving her a quick hug. THEY continue browsing.

Scene 3

Outside the supermarket. CHAD, GWEN and JASON enter, staying close to the edge of the stage.

CHAD
Okay, Jace, you just wait here. We'll be back in a second.

JASON
Are you sure I should stay here?

GWEN
Jason?

JASON
Yes, Ms Anderson?

GWEN
Shut up.

JASON
Yes, Ms Anderson.

DRIVE

CHAD crosses to stage centre and looks around.

                              CHAD

Okay, it's empty. Let's go.

                              GWEN

Positive?

                              CHAD

Yup. No cars in the carpark.

                              GWEN

Okay. (*to JASON*) Whatever happens, *stay here*.

                              JASON

But, what if something goes wrong?

                              GWEN

If something goes wrong then it's even *more* important you stay here. If the plan breaks, we'll need a quick getaway, not a hero.

JASON sighs loudly.

                              CHAD

Ready?

GWEN nods. THEY pull balaclavas over their heads and creep towards the entrance to the shop (offstage). THEY exit.

JASON creeps across stage. He follows GWEN and CHAD warily.

                              GWEN (O.S.)

Hands up! This is a hold up!

JASON trips off stage. CANS crash to the floor.

                              CHAD (O.S.)

Jason! What are you doing, man?

                              GWEN (O.S.)

Jason?

A crash.

DRIVE

GWEN (O.S.)

Get out of here!

A shot is fired.

The SHOPKEEPER groans off stage.

CHAD (O.S.)

He's hit! You shot him!

GWEN (O.S.)

Jason, get the hell out of here, *now*!

ACT VI

Scene 1

In the SUPERMARKET. NAOMI and ALEX huddle behind a row of SHELVES. KAITLAN huddles nearby.

On the other side of the stage, JASON is cradling the SHOPKEEPER, who is bleeding from a gun-wound to the shoulder. GWEN paces, and CHAD hovers nearby.

NAOMI

See? I told you this was a bad idea!

ALEX

What? No you didn't!

NAOMI

I did! I told you I shouldn't ever drive again! It just gets me into trouble!

ALEX

Naomi, don't be stupid. This has nothing to do with your driving.

NAOMI

Oh? So if I didn't drive, we'd still be here?

ALEX

Nome, /don't be

NAOMI

I'm not being silly! It's true, isn't it?

DRIVE

ALEX
Yeah, but it's backwards causation!

NAOMI
What?

ALEX
Backwards causation. You assume that just because thing b followed thing a, thing a caused thing b.

NAOMI
And? Didn't it?

ALEX
Oh, for Heaven's sake, girl, of course not! I seriously doubt that your decision to take the wheel influenced these crooks in their decision to rob the place.

KAITLAN *sniffles.*

NAOMI
Okay, so I might not have caused it, but we sure as heck wouldn't be here caught up in it if I hadn't gotten behind the wheel.

ALEX
Well, we are now. So we have to deal with it.

NAOMI
You're right. So, what are we going to do?

ALEX
How should I know?

NAOMI
You always know!

ALEX
No, I don't.

NAOMI
Sure you do! You're fix-it girl! No task is too big, no situation too scary, no misfortune too emotional to be practically overcome!

ALEX
Ah ha, funny.

NAOMI
I'm not trying to be funny. I'm trying to get you to tell me your plan.

ALEX
I don't have one.

NAOMI
Nothing?

ALEX
No.

NAOMI
Not at all?

ALEX
No.

Across stage, CHAD bumps into a SHELF, causing a loud crash.

ALEX and NAOMI jump.

ALEX
I got nothing, Nome. And I sure as heck hope you can come up with something quickly, 'cause I don't want to die here.

KAITLAN begins to cry.

NAOMI
Shh! You're scaring her. (*Moves towards KAITLAN*). Shh, now, it's okay, it's going to be okay. It's all going to be fine.

KAITLAN cries louder.

NAOMI pulls her close and cradles her in her lap.

NAOMI
Shh, shh there. Hush, hush.

ALEX
Can't you keep her quiet? I don't think they know we're here, and I'd rather not advertise our presence.

NAOMI
Alex! The poor girl is frightened half to death!

ALEX
Yeah, well, it might be more than half if they find out we're here.

KAITLAN shifts, knocking the shelf.

GWEN
What was that?

ALEX
Naomi? Naomi, I think they heard us. I think they know we're here...

GWEN moves closer.

GWEN
Hello?

ALEX
Naomi, she's coming closer! Naomi, what are we going to do, she knows we're here! They'll kill us, the police are right outside and we're going to die anyway!

KAITLAN sobs quietly.

NAOMI
Alex! *Shut up.* It's going to be okay!

ALEX
How? How is going to be okay? You don't know that, no one knows that. How do you know it's going to be okay?

NAOMI
Because you said so.

ALEX
(*still panicking*) What?

NAOMI
You said so. You told me there was a plan, remember?

ALEX
Oh, and what am I, God? You're going to take everything I say literally, now?

NAOMI
No. But I *am* going to take God literally. We're going to be okay.

GWEN creeps up to the SHELF and peers through.

GWEN

No! (*to CHAD*) You said this place was empty!

CHAD

What? It is!

GWEN

No, idiot, it isn't. (*She crosses back towards him*). There are three girls hiding behind those shelves over there.

CHAD

What? There can't be! I checked! There was no one in here!

GWEN

Well, obviously there was.

CHAD

But... But there weren't even any cars parked outside!

GWEN

Well, given the fact that they're practically *children*, perhaps, Chad, they didn't drive.

CHAD squirms. JASON looks sick, and tries to ignore the whole interchange, tending to the SHOPKEEPER'S wound.

CHAD

(*glances at the SHOPKEEPER*) Well, in for a penny, in for a pound, right?

GWEN

(*taps her lip thoughtfully*) What are you thinking?

CHAD

At this point, the police race in they're going to see the girls there and assume the worst, right?

GWEN nods.

CHAD

So, if we're going to get blamed for it anyway, we might as well use it, right?

JASON

Chad, I don't think /that's

DRIVE

CHAD
You never told me you planned on an *armed* hold up.

GWEN
Would it have changed things if I had?

JASON
YES!

CHAD
Probably not. But I would have been more careful. As it is, though, the shopkeeper's been shot... If they're going to do us in for armed hold-up, they won't think twice about throwing charges of holding hostages on top of that.

GWEN
And...

CHAD
And if we have them, we might as well use them. we might be able to get the police to give us some concessions if we let them go slowly, or something...

JASON
Chad, I *really* don't /think

GWEN
Chad, I like the way you think. Right, so what we'll do is...

ALEX
Naomi, what are we going to *do*? They've heard us, they know we're here, they were talking about *hostages*! We can't be hostages! I'm too young to be a hostage!

NAOMI
Alex, will you calm down?! We're going to be all right!

ALEX
We're not, we're going to die.

NAOMI
Alex. Shut up.

ALEX
(*deep breath*) Shutting up.

NAOMI
Good. Now. Here's what we're going to do. See that door back there?

ALEX
(*peers through shelves*) Yeah...

NAOMI
That's the door out back, right?

ALEX
How should I know?

NAOMI
Well, I'm assuming it is. Where else would it lead?

ALEX
Pit full of poisoned stakes, intertwined with king cobras?

NAOMI
Such happy thoughts. Thank you. Be serious will you?

ALEX
I was.

NAOMI gives her a Look.

ALEX
(*huffy sigh*) Oh, all right. Yes, I suppose it leads out the back. So what?

NAOMI
Well, presumably, that means it also leads to a back entrance, right?

ALEX
Maybe...

NAOMI
So all we have to do is sneak to the door, and we can escape. Right?

ALEX
...I don't know.

NAOMI
What do you mean, you don't know?

DRIVE

ALEX
How exactly do you plan to sneak to the door? Sounds pretty risky to me.

NAOMI
Riskier than sitting here, when they know we're here, and were planning things involving the word 'hostage'?

ALEX
(*beat*) Do you really think we can do it?

NAOMI
We can try.

ALEX
Trying could get us killed.

NAOMI
So could not trying. That's what you've been trying to tell me all along, isn't it?

ALEX
What?

NAOMI
Not trying, not living, can kill you just as easily as trying, and living, and doing things can.

ALEX
I said that?

NAOMI
Not in so many words...

Silence.

ALEX
(*to KAITLAN*) What do you think? Are you going to be able to sneak, or are you too terrified to move without yelping and giving us away?

NAOMI
Alex!

KAITLAN
I can do it. If she does.

NAOMI

Who, me?

KAITLAN nods.

ALEX

Well, Miss I'm-Too-Guilty-To-Be-Good-For-Anything, looks like you get to set that example after all. Happy?

NAOMI

Will you come with us?

ALEX

Fine. I'll come with you, and together we can all make a daring dash for freedom.

NAOMI

Then I'm happy. Okay, so, this is what we'll do...

ACT VII

Scene 1

In the SUPERMARKET. JASON still cradles the SHOPKEEPER. CHAD and GWEN are absorbed in an animated discussion.

NAOMI holds KAITLAN'S hand, ready to sneak towards the door.

NAOMI

Okay, Kaitlan, are you ready? Alex?

ALEX

Yeah, I'm ready.

NAOMI

Okay, good. Now What happens if they notice us?

ALEX makes eye contact, refusing to answer.

NAOMI

Kaitlan? What do you do if we're seen?

KAITLAN

We run back behind the shelves here and hide, and you'll come behind and make sure we're safe.

DRIVE

NAOMI
That's right.

ALEX
I don't see why you have to do it like that, Naomi.

NAOMI
Like what?

ALEX
Stop being so stubborn. You know like what. They have a gun. You could be killed.

NAOMI
Oh, so you're volunteering to run the negotiations, then?

ALEX
...It doesn't have to be *either* of us!

NAOMI
Well, I think it does.

ALEX
Yes, /but

NAOMI
You won't convince me otherwise, Lex. (*deep breath*) Can we just get on with this, please?

THEY *peer through the shelves at GWEN, CHAD and JASON.*

NAOMI
They seem pretty occupied. We need to go now, while they're not concentrating on us.

ALEX
Okay. (*to KAITLAN*) Ready?

KAITLAN
Yes. I'm following Naomi. I'm ready.

ALEX
Indeed. Okay, Nome, let's get out of here.

NAOMI
Let's.

NAOMI begins to sneak out behind the shelf, holding KAITLAN'S hand. ALEX holds KAITLAN'S other hand and follows them out.

KAITLAN brushes against the shelf and the ITEMS ON THE SHELF rattle. THEY freeze.

ALEX

Shh!

KAITLAN

I'm sorry! I didn't mean to!

NAOMI turns back to them and places a finger over her lips. THEY edge towards the door.

THEY are halfway there when GWEN abruptly ends her conversation with CHAD and stands. GWEN sees the escaping GIRLS.

GWEN

Hey! What do you think you're doing?

ALEX and KAITLAN dive behind the SHELF. An ORANGE falls off and rolls towards JASON, who glances at it periodically.

GWEN steps towards the SHELF.

NAOMI

Wait!

GWEN

What?

NAOMI

Wait, please! I... I want to talk to you.

GWEN

(*snorts*) Do you just.

NAOMI

(*swallows*) Yes.

GWEN

And why would that be?

NAOMI

I... I want to negotiate.

DRIVE

GWEN
Negotiate? With what? In case you're living in some little delusional bubble, sweetheart, we're the ones holding the guns.

NAOMI
Gun.

GWEN
What?

NAOMI
Gun, singular. You only have one.

GWEN
And you're sure of that, are you?

NAOMI
Yes. If the boys had had guns too they would have been wielding them. They *are* male, after all.

GWEN
(*hiding a grin*) Indeed. (*holsters her gun*). So. We have the gun. What do you have?

NAOMI
Influence.

GWEN
Influence? You're a teenage girl. How much influence do you honestly expect me to believe you have? Unless, of course, you have important parents. Do you?

NAOMI
Not especially.

GWEN
(*relaxes*) Well, what then? What is the 'influence' you have, and why on earth do I need it?

NAOMI
You didn't mean to shoot him.

GWEN
I... what?

NAOMI
You didn't mean to shoot the shopkeeper.

GWEN

(*dark look*) No. I didn't.

NAOMI

And you were surprised we were in here. I heard you yelling at that boy.

Silence, while GWEN processes what NAOMI is hinting at.

NAOMI

If you let us go, it'll be big points in your favour. The police will never believe you didn't know we were in here, and you'll be done for armed robbery, and holding hostages, and everything. If you let us go...

GWEN

On the other hand, if I keep you, I can use you to negotiate freedoms with the police.

NAOMI

Do you really expect that to work?

ALEX and KAITLAN bump the SHELF and it rattles.

GWEN glances over at the SHELF.

GWEN

(*mutters*) Excuse me.

NAOMI

No, wait!

GWEN brushes her aside.

NAOMI considers following, but turns to focus on the boys.

NAOMI

Hi. I'm Naomi. You don't have to do this, you know.

CHAD

Naomi, is it? Naomi, let me assure you of one thing: you have no idea what you're talking about.

CHAD turns his back on her and busies himself with the SHOPKEEPER.

NAOMI notices JASON glancing at the ORANGE, and picks it up.

DRIVE

                              NAOMI

Hungry?

JASON shakes his head, transfixed by the orange.

NAOMI looks back and forth between JASON and the ORANGE.

                              NAOMI

You don't have to do this, you know.

JASON blinks.

                              NAOMI

It's not too late.

                              CHAD

Look, girl, /you just

                              JASON

Yes, it is.

CHAD hesitates.

                              NAOMI

No, it isn't. Let us go. It'll show good-will, and I... I will testify that you didn't mean for the shopkeeper to get shot.

                              JASON

You... you will?

                              NAOMI

If you let us go.

                              JASON

I... I...

NAOMI holds the ORANGE out to JASON. He wants to take it, but can't bring himself to.

                              CHAD

She won't, man. She's just trying to get us to let her go.

                              NAOMI

I'm /not

                              CHAD

But regardless, you're talking to the wrong person, Naomi. He's not in charge here.

GWEN returns with ALEX and KAITLAN in tow.

GWEN

No. I am.

NAOMI

(*drops the ORANGE*) And? You didn't mean for anyone to get hurt. I bet you're all pretty decent people, even. Trust me, good people can make mistakes, /and

JASON

Oh yeah? And what would you know about mistakes?

NAOMI

I... I killed someone.

JASON and CHAD are visibly shocked. KAITLAN stares, but GWEN looks thoughtful.

NAOMI

It was... an accident.

CHAD

Oh, well, you see? That's completely diff/erent.

NAOMI

No, it's not. You didn't mean for him to get shot, did you? That was an accident too. And just because it's an accident doesn't make you any less responsible.

ALEX

Naomi...

NAOMI

You still did it, and it's still your fault, and if it wasn't for you the person would still be alive! I killed him, I killed him and it was *my fault*, not because I did anything wrong, but because I was in charge of the situation.

NAOMI spins to face GWEN, who raises her GUN instinctively. ALEX goes to jump out, but KAITLAN squeaks and holds her back.

NAOMI

(*at GWEN*) *I was in charge*. It was an accident, it was a kangaroo, and I couldn't have done anything different, but *I was in charge*, so it was *my fault*. The police aren't going to throw him (*gestures to JASON*) away for anywhere near as long as they will you, because you're in charge. Let us go. Please. It doesn't have to end like this.

NAOMI and GWEN stare at each other.

DRIVE

JASON stands.

JASON

Gwen?

GWEN and NAOMI continuing staring.

JASON

Gwen, I think she's right.

CHAD

Jace, /man

JASON

No, Chad. I think she's right. We shouldn't do this. We've done enough. (*picks up the ORANGE*). I think I'm going to go home now.

CHAD

What? You can't just leave! You promised, man! You promised you wouldn't bail!

GWEN

Stop. (*she freezes*). DUCK!

The doors crash open, smoke fills the room and the lights go out.

POLICEMAN 1

Everyone, freeze! Don't move! This is the police!

Appropriate sounds and yells as the POLICE enter and begin to rescue the HOSTAGES, and arrest the THEIVES.

Lights flicker on dimly. GWEN and CHAD have exited, and POLICE are exiting with ALEX and KAITLAN. JASON is still hunched over the SHOPKEEPER.

ALEX (O.S.)

Naomi! NAOMI!

NAOMI hesitates, watching JASON.

Three POLICEMAN enter. ONE hauls JASON to his feet and drags him away. The OTHER TWO put the SHOPKEEPER on a stretcher and exit.

NAOMI steps forward as if to say something.

JASON looks back, meets her eye, and nods. He exits with the POLICEMAN.

ALEX (O.S.)

Naomi!

NAOMI takes one last look, then exits.

ACT VIII

Scene 1

A POLICE STATION. NAOMI sits alone. Enter ALEX.

ALEX

Hey.

NAOMI

Oh, hey.

ALEX sits.

ALEX

So, how's things?

NAOMI

Fabulous. Nothing like a hostage situation to make life interesting, right?

ALEX

Ha ha. (*beat*) I was serious.

NAOMI

Actually, so was I. Kinda... puts things in perspective, right?

ALEX

Yeah.

Silence. ALEX notices KAITLAN and PARENTS (offstage).

ALEX

She seems okay, now.

NAOMI

Yeah, she looks good. That police woman did a great job of calming her down.

ALEX

Her parents seem like they were really worried about her.

DRIVE

                    NAOMI

Well, they would be, right?

                    ALEX

(*shrugs*) Mine just naturally assume I'll take care of myself.

                    NAOMI

Oh. That... kinda sucks.

                    ALEX

(*shrug*) They trust me. It's a good thing, really. (*beat*) It's the growing up thing that sucks, more.

                    NAOMI

How do you mean?

                    ALEX

Well, when you're little, you think it's going to be so great, right? So much freedom, you can do whatever you like, all that. And then you get there, and...

                    NAOMI

(*grin*) And it's not so free?

                    ALEX

(*grin*) Yeah, pretty much. It's that nasty word, 'responsibility'. Sure, you've got the freedom—but it comes with the responsibilities, and if you take the freedom, people naturally assume you're taking the responsibilities too...

                    NAOMI

Better than the other way around.

                    ALEX

'Spose so. Like what's-her-name, Tina's parents. Most responsible girl you could ever meet, but her parents don't trust her with *any*thing.

                    NAOMI

Exactly.

                    ALEX

My parents... well, I'm *glad* they trust me to look after myself—but I don't appear to very good at it, do I? I completely went to pieces under pressure, and that if it hadn't been for your quick thinking and calm talking, who knows what would have happened?

NAOMI
I just did what you would have /done.

ALEX
No, what *I* would have done, what I *did* do, is fall to pieces. (*beat*) I don't think I deserve my parents' trust.

NAOMI
Alex, that's nonsense.

ALEX
I /don't

NAOMI
No, honest, it is. How well do your parents know you, Alex?

ALEX
Pretty well, I guess...

NAOMI
Then don't you think they know you well enough to know if you can be trusted?

ALEX
But I stuffed up!

NAOMI
And? So did I! And if you don't mind me saying, I stuffed up significantly better than you did. *Your* stuff up didn't kill anyone. (*beat*) They trust you, Alex, and I trust you; to calm me down, to knock sense into me when I spend months moping over *my* mistakes... And God trusts you, right?

ALEX
I... guess so. I don't know why.

NAOMI
Alex? Join the club.

ALEX'S MOBILE PHONE rings.

ALEX
Hello? Yeah, sure. No problem. Bye. (*turns to NAOMI*) It's my parents. They've come to pick me up. I better go.

DRIVE

NAOMI
See? They care about you.

ALEX
Yeah. Yeah, I know they do.

ALEX exits.

As NAOMI leans back to close her eyes, KAREN enters and sits beside NAOMI.

KAREN
So, you finally got back in the driver's seat.

NAOMI
Huh. And turned it into yet another fiasco.

KAREN
A fiasco that you dug yourself out of quite well, as I understand it.

NAOMI
Maybe.

KAREN
Well, I'm proud of you, Naomi. You have to drive your own life, after all, and I'm pleased to see you've taken the wheel again.

NAOMI
I don't get it. I thought the whole point was that we were supposed to put God in the driver's seat, or something?

KAREN
In a way, yes.

NAOMI
But in a way, no?

KAREN
Exactly.

NAOMI
Confused.

KAREN
It's like this. When you were growing up, did you ever drive yourself places?

NAOMI

What?

KAREN

I drove for you, right?

NAOMI

I guess so.

KAREN

But then, one day you got old enough to get your L plates, yes?

NAOMI

Yeah.

KAREN

And you started driving. Of course, I was right there with you while you were learning, but eventually, you've learned to drive yourself.

NAOMI

I still don't get what that has to do with—

KAREN

Our relationship with God is so much like parent and child, Naomi. It starts out with Him driving our lives for us, but as we get older, as we grow in faith, He begins to teach us what it means to drive ourselves—and one day, He hands us the keys. He lets us go, trusting that we've learned from Him what we can, and that we will follow His principles and apply them to our lives. Just like a parent, He hopes we'll do the job he's equipped us for—the job He's entrusted to us.

NAOMI

You raised me for a job?

KAREN

I did. All parents do, I think, whether they know it or not.

NAOMI

Mind telling me what it is?

KAREN

You want to know what I raised you to do? I raised you to be the best person you could be, to be true to yourself and to others, and to walk by faith.

NAOMI
That's it? That's my job?

KAREN
You sound disappointed.

NAOMI
No, it's just... Well, it's not very *specific*, is it?

KAREN
That's the frustrating thing about trust. When you're big enough to be trusted, often what you're trusted *with* is the task of figuring life out for yourself.

NAOMI
But I thought God was supposed to help us, to guide us?

KAREN
He does, just like I help and guide you. But that doesn't mean He'll run your life for you, any more than I will. God trusts you, Naomi. Now trust Him, and trust yourself.

NAOMI
(*murmurs*) But I'm not trustworthy.

KAREN
What?

NAOMI
Nothing. It's just something Alex said. "I'm not trustworthy," she said.

KAREN
Ultimately, I don't think any of us are.

NAOMI
Then why does God place so much trust in us? When He knows we're going to fail?

KAREN
We fail when we do it alone, Naomi. God doesn't misplace His trust—He equips us to live up to it. All we have to do it ask.

Scene 2

A POLICE HOLDING CELL. JASON sits on a BUNK, head in hands.

His FATHER enters, holding a PEELED ORANGE.

FATHER
Catch.

JASON catches the ORANGE and stares at it.

JASON
I was ten the last time you peeled one for me. You used to do it all the time. *(beat)* Why did you stop?

FATHER
You were ten the last time you asked me to.

Silence.

FATHER crosses the room and sits on the BUNK.

FATHER
(gestures to ORANGE) May I?

JASON
Sure.

FATHER eats a slice.

FATHER
Good orange. Want some? No? Why? Because I offered it to you?

FATHER eats another slice or two.

FATHER
So. I have a dilemma.

JASON
Mm?

FATHER
Well, it's your birthday next week, right?

JASON nods.

FATHER
And I had this wonderful present all lined up for you. But now...

DRIVE

JASON hangs his head.

JASON
I'm sorry, Dad.

FATHER
Really? Why is that?

JASON
For... for everything! What do you mean, why is that? I'm in a police cell, Dad, and they didn't just put me here because I looked at them funny! Surely they told you what happened.

FATHER
Perhaps. But for now, that issue is not relevant.

JASON
Not relevant? What do /you mean, not

FATHER
As I was saying, I have a dilemma. You see, I had a birthday present all picked out for you, as good as paid for, and I was just awaiting delivery. But the problem is, someone appears to have stolen it.

JASON
Someone stole... my birthday present?

FATHER
Indeed they did, Jason. Indeed they did.

Silence as FATHER eats more ORANGE.

JASON
Dad?

FATHER
Mmm?

JASON
What... What was my present?

FATHER
Are you sure you want to know?

JASON nods.

FATHER
You won't be crushingly disappointed, even knowing that someone has stolen it from you?

JASON shakes his head.

FATHER
It was a (specific car description).

JASON
No...

FATHER
Yes, indeed. The (colour) one down at (nameofcardealer)'s.

JASON
No... No, you can't have...

FATHER
Indeed, I most certainly could have. You've been going on about that car for months, now. Do you think I'm deaf?

JASON
Dad... why? I mean, why did you have to get me the car?

FATHER
What, you didn't actually want it?

JASON
No, I...

FATHER
Then what? You made it clear you wanted it, and I got an excellent bonus at work recently, and as work has been keeping me away from you so much lately, I thought it was only fair that you should benefit from the money. So I bought it for you. Is there a problem with that? Other, that is, than the fact that it has been stolen?

FATHER resumes his orange-eating.

JASON
Dad?

FATHER
Mmm?

DRIVE

JASON

It... It was me. I stole the car.

FATHER *appears to ignore him, and finishes all of the ORANGE except one piece.*

JASON

Dad?

FATHER *licks his fingers clean.*

JASON

Dad, please, say something!

FATHER

(*looks him directly in the eye*) All right. I'll say something. I trust you, Jason, to find a way out of this mess. I am here to help you—*if you ask*. Just as I have been there for you, your entire life—*whenever you asked*. Just like, with the car, you *only needed* to ask.

JASON

But... But... I've been asking for *months*, and you never even seemed to hear me! You were always running out the door, late for a meeting or late for work or needing to get to work early—always, too busy to even listen to me!

FATHER

I'm sorry if it seemed that way. This has been a busy few months. But I think these (*he pulls out a set of KEYS from his pocket*) demonstrate that I was listening, wouldn't you agree?

JASON

What are they?

FATHER

The keys to your car.

JASON

My... car?

FATHER

Well, I paid for it before you so kindly thought to remove it from the showroom for me, so I've been able to convince the dealership it was nothing more than a rather large misunderstanding.

JASON

You... have?

FATHER
Indeed.

JASON
Um, thank you! (*He reaches for the KEYS*)

FATHER
(*jerking the KEYS back*) Have you heard a word I've been saying to you?

JASON
(*grinning*) Dad?

FATHER
Yes, son?

JASON
Can I have the keys?

FATHER
(*gravely*) Yes. Yes you can. Once you have paid back your debt to society.

JASON
What? But I /thought

FATHER
What? That I would pick up the pieces and let you walk away from your messes? And what kind of parent would that make me? No. It doesn't work like that, I'm afraid.

JASON
Oh.

FATHER
(*gently*) Maybe, next time, it might be worth waiting to see what I have in store for you?

JASON
(*flat*) Maybe.

FATHER
Jason, you are my only son. I would die for you. And I raised you to be a good boy, to be someone I could trust. I can still trust you, right?

JASON
(*half smile*) Right.

DRIVE

FATHER

Jason?

JASON

Mm?

FATHER

I trust you. Now, trust me.

Slowly, JASON smiles, then leans towards his FATHER.

JASON

Dad?

FATHER

Yes, son?

JASON

Dad, can I have some orange?

FATHER

I thought you'd never ask.

WHERE YOUR TREASURE IS

When the king issues a decree telling the local pirates to accept his quest for treasure or be hanged for traitors, there is mass disbelief. But Calico Jack and his first mate Shark Tooth decide to take up the quest, followed by the odious Squid Lips Sid and his mate Decayin' Dave, who hope to steal the treasure out from under them.

But things don't go according to plan. The map that Shark Tooth has procured is vague and feels totally unhelpful. The journey is long and hard. And when Calico Jack and Shark Tooth finally discover the treasure, it's not at all what they expected: there's no gold, no silver—just the king's missing son.

Squid Lips Sid and Decayin' Dave arrive to try to steal the treasure, and the king's son is shot protecting Calico Jack and Shark Tooth. Terrified, Calico Jack and Shark Tooth decide to return the body to the king regardless—at any rate it might prevent them from hanging. To their surprise and delight, the king not only resurrects his son, but offers the two pirates a place in his family.

ACTORS REQUIRED

Male
6*

Female
0

Either
2

MINIMUM TOTAL
6

*Although the main pirate roles are scripted as male, the original performance of this play successfully cast DECAYIN' DAVE and SHARK TOOTH as female.

WHERE YOUR TREASURE IS

SCENE SUMMARIES

ACT I

SCENE 1
The King issues a challenge to the Pirates, whom he has just overcome in battle: find his treasure and receive his pardon, or be hanged as criminals.

SCENE 2
Shark Tooth and Calico Jack, odd map in hand, set out to find the treasure.

ACT II

SCENE 1
As they gradually figure out how the odd map works, Calico Jack and Shark Tooth determine they are on the right path after all.

SCENE 2
Squid Lips Sid and Decayin' Dave spot Calico Jack and Shark Tooth and decide to follow them so they can steal the treasure.

SCENE 3
In the Swamp of the Despair, the pirates all nearly give up, until Calico Jack realises it's the swamp influencing their decisions.

ACT III

SCENE 1
Calico Jack and Shark Tooth find the treasure and narrowly escape having it stolen by Squid Lips Sid and Decayin' Dave—only to discover it isn't what they were expecting.

WHERE YOUR TREASURE IS

ACT IV

SCENE 1

Calico Jack and Shark Tooth head back to the castle, only to be attacked in the Valley of the Shadow of Death by Squid Lips Sid and Decayin' Dave. The king's son dies protecting them.

ACT V

SCENE 1

Calico Jack and Shark Tooth arrive at the castle bearing the body of the king's son, and to their surprise are welcomed by the king. The king resurrects his son and welcomes the pirates into his family.

WHERE YOUR TREASURE IS

CAST OF CHARACTERS

DECAYIN' DAVE
A pirate. Not so clever; bumbling and a little slow on the uptake.

SQUID LIPS SID
A pirate. Large and bulky. A bully.

CALICO JACK
A pirate captain. Smart enough, a decent fellow, but likely to get carried away on points of honour.

SHARK TOOTH
Calico Jack's first mate. Sensible, cynical, intelligent, practical.

SON
The son of the King and heir to the throne. In bad shape.

KING
The King of the land. A fair, just and rather cunning ruler.

HERALD
A messenger sent from the king. Haughty and proud, thinks he's well above the pirates.

PIRATE ONE
An extra.

WHERE YOUR TREASURE IS

ACT I

Scene 1

A pirate gathering. PIRATES lounge around the set, and CALICO JACK and SHARK TOOTH sit together front centre stage.

Enter the King's HERALD.

HERALD
(*clears throat*) A message from the King, to the pirates of this place.

PIRATES cease games and chatter to listen. Throughout the HERALD's speech they mutter and interject rudely.

HERALD
The battle is over, the war is won, and I have been proclaimed the rightful king. Henceforth, piracy is outlawed. Any man condemned of piracy shall be hanged by the neck until dead.

PIRATES are outraged.

HERALD
My men will wipe the country clean of the last of your number. We will hunt you down like a dog hunts rats, and tear you apart with equal fury. But I am not without mercy. I make to you this proposition
If you accept my terms, then you shall be pardoned, and allowed to go free.

PIRATES in uproar.

PIRATE ONE
Terms? We don't want no terms!

DECAYIN' DAVE
We'll kill ye where ye stand!

WHERE YOUR TREASURE IS

PIRATES roar in agreement and move to attack the HERALD.

SQUID LIPS SID
Get 'im, mateys! Kill 'im dead!

CALICO JACK
Stop!

PIRATES freeze.

SHARK TOOTH
What's wrong?

CALICO JACK
Let's hear what this herald has to say. What're the terms, matey?

SQUID LIPS SID
We don't need to hear no terms! We don't none of us wants to be consortin' with the "king" anyhow.

DECAYIN' DAVE
Aye, that we don't!

PIRATE ONE
I say kill 'im!

CALICO JACK
And I say let's hear him out. Or does any man of ye want to be disputing that with me?

PIRATES back away begrudgingly.

CALICO JACK
If ye please.

HERALD
(*straightening himself out, he mumbles to find his place again*) ...allowed to go free. (*louder*) These are my terms: that whoever among you wishes to be considered for a pardon must agree to undertake my quest, that you shall commit to it wholeheartedly and swear not to deviate from it in the slightest, that you will fight and overcome any obstacles that you may encounter, and that you will succeed in the task I set before you.

SQUID LIPS SID
Do ye have to take half an hour to get the point? What d' we have to do?

SHARK TOOTH
Quiet, matey, he'll be coming to that next. You know how the king is, with all his fancy language.

DECAYIN' DAVE
Aye, he likes to sound like he's smart, but really we all know he's just making stuff up.

PIRATES roar in assent.

CALICO JACK
Shush! Herald, continue.

HERALD
Hmph. Your quest is thus: find my treasure. For where my treasure is, there also is my heart, and he who has my heart has my pardon. (*rolls up the PROCLAMATION*)

SQUID LIPS SID
That's it? Find his treasure?

DECAYIN' DAVE
I don't trust 'im. Something about this stinks.

SHARK TOOTH
Nay, that'd be you, Decayin' Dave.

PIRATES laugh.

DECAYIN' DAVE
All I'm sayin' is, why'd the king be letting us off these here charges of 'piracy' just fer findin' his treasure?

SQUID LIPS SID
Sounds like a good deal to me. We accept kingo's terms, get directions to the treasure, then when we find it take it for ourselves!

SHARK TOOTH
And you'd get so far with it with the king's proclamation hanging over your head. Or, sorry, with your head hanging over the king's proclamation.

SQUID LIPS SID glances at the HERALD, who harrumps and looks down his nose at everyone.

SQUID LIPS SID
(*grumbling*) Fine. New plan. (*to Decayin' Dave*) What do you think? You up for some treasure hunting?

WHERE YOUR TREASURE IS

                                  DECAYIN' DAVE

Better a treasure hunt than a dead man's noose.

                                  SQUID LIPS SID

(*to HERALD*) Right. We're in then. Where's the treasure map?

                                  HERALD

Map? Who said anything about a map?

                                  DECAYIN' DAVE

(*astonished*) But how are we supposed to find the treasure without a map?

                                  SQUID LIPS SID

(*grabs HERALD by the shirt*) Yeah, smarty pants. Tell us how we're supposed to find the treasure if we don't know what it is or where to look for it. Huh? Huh?

HERALD squeaks.

                                  CALICO JACK

Put him down, Squid Lips, ye big bully.

                                  SQUID LIPS SID

Oo, looky here. It's Calico Jack to the rescue. Why d'ye want to save this miserable squealer anyway? (*shakes HERALD*) Yer not in league with the king's men, are ye?

                                  SHARK TOOTH

Squid Lips, you buffoon, Jack just lost his ship because the navy blasted it out of the water. Half his crew are visiting Davy Jones. Why'd they do that if he was in league with them?

                                  SQUID LIPS SID

Maybe he betrayed his crew.

                                  SHARK TOOTH

Or maybe, ye big lummox, he's sensible enough to know that if ye kill one o'the king's men, ye'll be the first to hang.

                                  CALICO JACK

(*tears SQUID LIPS SID away from HERALD*) Let him go. (*to HERALD*) But look, you. Squid Lips may have the brains of half a jellyfish up a tree, but he's got a point. If we were to accept yer terms—and I'm not saying we are—where would we go t' start looking?

HERALD
(*straightening coat*) If you allow me, Sir, to finish, your fears shall be allayed. The king has no map, for his treasure has been stolen.

PIRATES in uproar.

HERALD
BUT he has these clues for you. Firstly, be careful what you seek. Secondly, those who seek shall find. Thirdly, find your heart—for where your heart is, there is your treasure.

SQUID LIPS SID
Useless! Utterly useless! I say we kill 'im after all! (*attacks the HERALD*)

SHARK TOOTH
(*to CALICO JACK*) Aren't you going to stop him?

CALICO JACK
Well, you have to admit. The clues were a bit obscure. Still. I suppose you're right.

CALICO JACK draws his SWORD and attacks SQUID LIPS SID. SQUID LIPS SID roars and turns to fend off the attack.

The PIRATES all break out in a brawl, and HERALD escapes.

SHARK TOOTH

(*aside*) Well, isn't this interesting, the king offering us all a pardon. Why trust a bunch of thieving pirates to hunt down his treasure for him? And where do you start looking when your only clue is 'find your heart'? What've hearts got to do with treasure, anyway? A heart is only good while it's beating in your chest. You can't hoarde it or sell it or trade it for riches. (*glances at fight*) I'd better pull Jack out of there before he takes someone's arm off. He's a good man, a good captain, but he does like to make his point. (*shouting into CALICO JACK'S ear*) Come on, Jack. Let's leave these scarecrows to their brawling.

CALICO JACK
Aye, but pirates never leave a fight, Shark Tooth me matey.

SHARK TOOTH
(*dodging the blows of other pirates*) Not true, Captain. They that are brainless leave when they are dead. They that are wise leave before.

CALICO JACK
Sod it all. All right, I'm coming. (*extricates himself from the fight by sending his opponent chasing after someone else*) There. Be ye happy?

WHERE YOUR TREASURE IS

SHARK TOOTH

I'd be happier if there weren't a noose around my neck about to draw in tight.

CALICO JACK

You want to go after the treasure.

SHARK TOOTH nods.

CALICO JACK

You think we can find it?

SHARK TOOTH

Calico Jack and good old Shark Tooth? We can do anything, Captain.

CALICO JACK

True enough, me matey, true enough. Well, then. Let's say I indulge you this once. Where do you propose to start?

SHARK TOOTH

(*fishes out MAP*) I say we start here, on the map.

CALICO JACK

Where in the name of the seven seas did you procure yeself a map? The herald said as there was none!

SHARK TOOTH

Heralds, like pirates, lie. I fished it out of his pocket as I sent him out the door.

CALICO JACK

Why, Shark Tooth, ye be worth more than yer weight in gold. I do applaud ye.

SQUID LIPS SID

(*over CALICO JACK and SHARK TOOTH's shoulders*) What're you two up to?

SHARK TOOTH

None o' yer business, Squid Lips. Go back to yer fight, no one's cut yer head off yet.

SQUID LIPS SID

Why you...

SQUID LIPS SID tries to grab SHARK TOOTH but CALICO JACK fends him off.

SQUID LIPS SID

(*to CALICO JACK, nastily*) So, I suppose you're going to have a go at the king's treasure hunt, then?

CALICO JACK

Maybe.

SQUID LIPS SID

Maybe? Ye can't help yeself. Always wanted to be a grand hero, ye did. Well, I tell ye what
this time ye 'll have a battle on ye hands, Calico. Me and Decayin' Dave, we're plannin' to take up this king's quest, and we'll beat ye all t' the treasure!

SHARK TOOTH

And what'll you do with it then?

SQUID LIPS SID

Take it for—

SHARK TOOTH mimes hanging from a noose.

SQUID LIPS SID

—for th' king, o' course.

SHARK TOOTH

Yeah, well, good fer you. Now if you'll excuse us, we have business to attend to. (*shoulders SQUID LIPS aside and fluffs out the MAP*)

SQUID LIPS SID

What's that?

CALICO JACK

Nothing.

SQUID LIPS SID

Looks t' me like a map!

CALICO JACK

Do I need to run you through with my sword?

SQUID LIPS SID

Ahhrr, ye think ye're so tough, Calico Jack, but we'll see who's hangin' at the end of the day. We'll see. (*returns to the fight and drags DECAYIN' DAVE away, exiting during SHARK TOOTH and CALICO JACK's exchange*)

SHARK TOOTH

We'll have trouble with that one.

WHERE YOUR TREASURE IS

CALICO JACK
Eh, we've done trouble before.

SHARK TOOTH
Not for such high stakes.

CALICO JACK
Ah, Shark Tooth, me matey. Ye've gots to go sometime. All the same, I'd rather it not be at the mercy of the hangman. So we'll look for this treasure of yours—or else die trying.

SHARK TOOTH
It isn't my treasure.

CALICO JACK
Ye've got the map, lad. That makes it yours. Come on. Let's leave these bilge rats to their bickering.

CALICO JACK and SHARK TOOTH exit.

<u>Scene 2</u>

SHARK TOOTH's room in their temporary on-shore quarters. SHARK TOOTH is examining the map. Enter CALICO JACK.

CALICO JACK
Ahoy there.

SHARK TOOTH
Ahoy.

CALICO JACK
So. Have ye found anything that be of use?

SHARK TOOTH
(*wryly*) Not so much.

CALICO JACK
But it's a map! Surely it gives us some starting point for the hunt?

SHARK TOOTH
(*showing CALICO JACK the map*) Look here.

CALICO JACK
Aye, it's a map. There's a starting point, and a dotted trail, and clues, and see there, a big X.

SHARK TOOTH
Look at the clues.

CALICO JACK
Go ye first to the Hill of Difficulty, and learn to persevere.

SHARK TOOTH
And the next one.

CALICO JACK
Do not let your motivation falter by the Languishing Lagoon.

SHARK TOOTH
See what I mean? Rubbish. They're all rubbish. No use at all.

CALICO JACK
Arrh, but that's where ye be wrong. They do be of use.

SHARK TOOTH
How? Fer fooling us so's we can't complete the quest? King would be happy then, he'd get to hang us all.

CALICO JACK
Nay, Shark Tooth, though who's to say if ye're right or wrong. I mean, at least we know the names o' the places we're going!

SHARK TOOTH opens his mouth but can't refute the point.

CALICO JACK
See? (*claps SHARK TOOTH on the shoulder*) So! Away, me hearty. Let's head us towards the Hill of Difficulty!

CALICO JACK exits cheerily. SHARK TOOTH follows dubiously.

ACT II

Scene 1

CALICO JACK and SHARK TOOTH in the jungle with the MAP.

WHERE YOUR TREASURE IS

SHARK TOOTH
Look, no, it's this way. The map goes up this way.

CALICO JACK
I don't think so. This arrow clearly means 'north'.

SHARK TOOTH
Yes, just like the lake clearly marked a lake and the hill clearly marked a hill?

CALICO JACK
Well, it was kind of a lake. We got wet.

SHARK TOOTH
We got wet because you fell asleep while you were walking and slipped right in!

CALICO JACK
Avast, scoundrel! Ye fell in right behind me!

SHARK TOOTH
Only to pull you out!

CALICO JACK
Well... Okay, but the hill was definitely a hill.

SHARK TOOTH
How can you say that? It was perfectly flat ground!

CALICO JACK
Yes, but we had an uphill battle, didn't we?

SHARK TOOTH groans.

CALICO JACK
Well, it was! What did the clue on the map say again?

SHARK TOOTH
Go to the Hill of Difficulty and learn to persevere.

CALICO JACK
Well, see! We did! Perseverance ahoy! Clearly we're on the right track.

SHARK TOOTH

Fantasic, so we can expect the Swamp of Despair next? I bet I know exactly what that will be like awful. We'll wade through muck and scum and get depressed about the whole thing and wonder why we're even bothering. So—why bother?

CALICO JACK

Because we're treasure hunting!

SHARK TOOTH

Hmph. You really trust the king?

CALICO JACK

Sure, why not?

SHARK TOOTH

Because he's the king, that's why! We make a living out of breaking his laws! Why would he want to help us?

CALICO JACK

I haven't the foggiest. What did that herald say?

SHARK TOOTH

You mean there was meaning beneath all those fancy words?

CALICO JACK

King says he's the merciful type, doesn't he? So, you know. Maybe he doesn't like havin' t' kill all the pirates.

SHARK TOOTH

So why'd he outlaw it, then?

CALICO JACK

Rules is rules.

SHARK TOOTH

He's the king! He could change the rules if he liked.

CALICO JACK

Ah, but then where would that stop? You change one rule to suit yerself, what's to stop you changing them all?

SHARK TOOTH

Nothing, he's the king.

WHERE YOUR TREASURE IS

                              CALICO JACK
Right, and we're pirates, and even we live by a code. Things'd be chaos, otherwise.

                              SHARK TOOTH
So you trust the king's that there's going to be treasure, simply because he said he was trustworthy?

                              CALICO JACK
...Yes?

                              SHARK TOOTH
I despair.

                              CALICO JACK
Ah ha! See? We're in the right place! Swamp o' Despair!

                              SHARK TOOTH
You're incorrigible.

                              CALICO JACK
It's treasure. Besides, you're the one who started us on this little quest.

                              SHARK TOOTH
(*sigh*) Okay. Swamp of Despair it is. Yuck.

SHARK TOOTH and CALICO JACK exit.

                              <u>Scene 2</u>

SQUID LIPS SID and DECAYIN' DAVE in the jungle.

                              SQUID LIPS SID
Wait! I hear something.

They listen.

                              DECAYIN' DAVE
Sounds like people.

                              SQUID LIPS SID
(*malicious grin*) Why, it be more than that. Sounds like Calico Jack and his Toothless Shark t' me.

DECAYIN' DAVE
Shiver me timbers! Let's get a-going!

SQUID LIPS SID
Nay, Decayin' Dave. I has me a better plan. Them scurvy dogs has a map, remember?

DECAYIN' DAVE
I saw it, I did, when they was leaving the old hut, and they was creepin' around all secret-like, and Shark Tooth, I mean the Toothless Shark, he was holding it all careful-like until he tripped and nearly dropped it, and then I saw it, and—

SQUID LIPS SID
Avast ye with yer chatting, scallyway, or I'll feed ye to the fishes.

DECAYIN' DAVE
(*salutes*) Yes, Cap'n Squid Lips, sir!

SQUID LIPS SID
Stop that! Anyways, I have a plan. They have a map, right?

DECAYIN' DAVE
Right, because I saw it, and—

SQUID LIPS SID
Dave?

DECAYIN' DAVE
Yes, sir, Squid Lips, Sir?

SQUID LIPS SID
Shut up.

DECAYIN' DAVE
Yes sir, shutting up, sir. I'm the shuttiest up pirate what did ever roam the seven seas!

SQUID LIPS SID
Ye'll be roaming them from the inside of a fish's belly if you don't quit now!

DECAYIN' DAVE mimes close his lips.

SQUID LIPS SID
Right. So. They have a map, and we don't. So what do we do?

Looks at DECAYIN' DAVE, but D. DAVE can't talk because his lips are still sealed.

WHERE YOUR TREASURE IS

SQUID LIPS SID
(*gritting teeth*) We follow them, of course.

D. DAVE bounces.

SQUID LIPS SID
Dave, ye're the thickest Son of a Biscuit Eater in th' whole world. Can ye keep quiet while we follow them, do you think?

D. DAVE bounces some more and points to his sealed lips.

SQUID LIPS SID
Aye, well, see that you do stay quiet, or I'll keelhaul y' and feed y' to the fishes when I'm done. Now. You stay here while I go find out what they're up to. Stay put, savvy?

D. DAVE nods enthusiastically.

SQUID LIPS SID exits.

After a moment, D. DAVE grows fretful. He exits after SQUID LIPS SID.

Scene 3

A swamp.

SHARK TOOTH
Jack, this is impossible. I refuse to go a step further.

CALICO JACK
Come on, me hearty. Ye can do it!

SHARK TOOTH
So what if I can? What's the point? I'm tired, I'm hungry, and I'm up to my neck in muck and mosquitos.

CALICO JACK
But it's treasure hunting! That's what happens!

SHARK TOOTH
Not in the stories. In the stories treasure hunting is glamorous and exciting and you actually find treasure.

CALICO JACK
We'll find the treasure.

SHARK TOOTH

Pah. We don't even know we're in the right place. I give up.

CALICO JACK

...You know what? I do too.

SHARK TOOTH

You do?

CALICO JACK

Yes. I'm sick of you whinging all the time, of having to be the happy and upbeat pirate. I want a turn at being negative for a change.

SHARK TOOTH

I am not negative!

CALICO JACK

You're always negative. So. There it is. We quit.

CALICO JACK and SHARK TOOTH flop to the ground.

DECAYIN' DAVE

Oh, no! What're we going to do, Squid Lips? If they quit we won't be able to follow them!

SQUID LIPS SID

I knew this idea of yours was a bad one!

DECAYIN' DAVE

My idea? This was my idea?

SQUID LIPS SID

Of course it was. You don't think I'd come up with such a stinking plan, do you?

DECAYIN' DAVE

Well, I—

SQUID LIPS SID

Of course not. So it has to have been your idea.

DECAYIN' DAVE

Oh. Okay. Well, in that case, my ideas stinks. I vote we quit.

WHERE YOUR TREASURE IS

SQUID LIPS SID
Yeah. These blundering idiots couldn't lead us to the treasure if they tried, anyway.

D. DAVE and SQUID LIPS SID also sink to the ground.

CALICO JACK
Shark Tooth, I've just remembered something. Pass me the map. (*examines map*) Ha! See here! The swamp.

SHARK TOOTH
You needed the map to know we were in a swamp? Were the mud and flies not enough?

CALICO JACK
No, look at the name.

SHARK TOOTH
Swamp of Despair. How apt. I do despair indeed.

CALICO JACK
We both did. But don't ye see? Read them clues again.

SHARK TOOTH
In the Swamp of Despair, do not fall down to the depths. Helpful, since I see no depths to fall into. Unless you think the grass is hiding something. (*pokes around*) Hidden trapdoor, maybe?

CALICO JACK
Ye're taking it too literally. Think about them other clues, like the Hill of Difficulty, where there was no hill to be seen.

SHARK TOOTH
...Fine. So. Depths... The depths of despair...

CALICO JACK
That's it!

SHARK TOOTH
What's it?

CALICO JACK
The depths of despair. Do not let yourself fall into the depths of despair, is what it means.

SHARK TOOTH

Why not? We're stuck in the middle of a swamp. I think a little negative feeling is appropriate.

CALICO JACK

But not despair. Despair means giving up, quitting. It means ye have no hope whatsoever.

SHARK TOOTH

And that is not a perfectly apt description of us because...?

CALICO JACK

The other clues. The ones the herald gave. Be careful what ye seek, for what ye seek ye'll find.

SHARK TOOTH

You don't really believe that, do you?

CALICO JACK

Yes, I do.

SHARK TOOTH

But... why? It's not logical!

CALICO JACK

Neither is a swamp of despair, and yet here we are. We have to keep going, Shark Tooth.

SHARK TOOTH

Yeah, well. Don't get too excited. Remember the last clue? "Find your heart, for where your heart is, there is your treasure." What about that? It's utter rubbish!

CALICO JACK

Maybe. Or... maybe we just don't understand it yet. But should we let the fact that we can't understand one part keep us from following the parts that we do?

SHARK TOOTH

But how can you be sure the whole thing is logical if you don't understand it all?

CALICO JACK

I don't need to understand it all to know that the bit I do understand makes sense. Be careful what you seek; what you seek you'll find. I'm seeking the treasure. (*beat*) Besides, who knows? Maybe I'm just working backwards, and I'll find my heart when I find the treasure.

WHERE YOUR TREASURE IS

                              SHARK TOOTH

Do you even know what you just said?

                              CALICO JACK

Nope. (*grins*) But it got you on your feet, didn't it?

                              SHARK TOOTH

(*sighs*) Come on, then. Scoundrel. Get a move on.

SHARK TOOTH follows CALICO JACK away.

D. DAVE snaps out of his reverie and shakes SQUID LIPS SID.

                              DECAYIN' DAVE

Sid! Squid lips! Sid, wake up, they're moving on.

                              SQUID LIPS SID

Hmm? Wha?

                              DECAYIN' DAVE

They're moving again. Are we going to follow them?

                              SQUID LIPS SID

I'd rather sleep.

                              DECAYIN' DAVE

But what about the treasure?

                              SQUID LIPS SID

(*finally fully awake*) Treasure? Where?

                              DECAYIN' DAVE

That way. Quick, let's follow them.

                              SQUID LIPS SID

Ha. I knew my idea would work in the end. Come on. After them!

Exit SQUID LIPS SID and DECAYIN' DAVE in pursuit of SHARK TOOTH and CALICO JACK.

ACT III

Scene 1

A clearing in the jungle. An OLD SEA CHEST is half buried centre stage.

Enter CALICO JACK and SHARK TOOTH.

CALICO JACK

Treasure ahoy! We did it, me matey!

SHARK TOOTH

So it appears.

CALICO JACK

Ahrr, don't be so suspicious. There's the treasure chest, right there!

SHARK TOOTH

Yes, but it's where the map said it would be.

CALICO JACK

So? Isn't that how a treasure map's supposed to work?

SHARK TOOTH

Yes. But this isn't a treasure map. (*ticks off on fingers*) The lake that wasn't a lake, the hill that wasn't a hill, the swamp that wasn't a swamp, the—

CALICO JACK

All right, I get the point. Well. Let's open this treasure, then, shall we?

SQUID LIPS SID and DECAYIN' DAVE burst onto the scene, swords at the ready.

SQUID LIPS SID

Avast, ye blackhearted dogs!

DECAYIN' DAVE

Stop where ye stand!

SHARK TOOTH

Oh, look! The little pretend pirates think they're going to rob us of our treasure.

SQUID LIPS SID

Pretend? Pretend?

WHERE YOUR TREASURE IS

                              SHARK TOOTH

Aw, now they think they're parrots. How cute.

                              SQUID LIPS SID

Why, you! I'll kill you where you stand!

                              CALICO JACK

Shark Tooth, stop baiting them. You know perfectly well they're not going to steal anything off us.

                              SQUID LIPS SID

Wanna bet?

                              DECAYIN' DAVE

Yeah, wanna bet?

                              SHARK TOOTH

(*raises eyebrow*) Depends. How much have you got to wager? Because we have this chest chock full of treasure, you see, and I don't know you could afford to bet with us.

                              SQUID LIPS SID

Scoundrel, it's our treasure! We're stealing it from you, fair and square! Dave, go!

SQUID LIPS SID and DECAYIN' DAVE lunge at the treasure.

CALICO JACK and SHARK TOOTH dive in to protect it.

They fight.

CALICO JACK and SHARK TOOTH hold the other two off, but only just.

                              CALICO JACK

Stop! Stop all of you. Let's see if we can't come to some sort of... arrangement.

                              SHARK TOOTH

Like what? They go away and never bother us again, and we take our treasure and skedaddle?

                              CALICO JACK

I was thinking more along the lines of sharing the reward.

                              SQUID LIPS SID

Sharing?

DECAYIN' DAVE
Sharing?

SHARK TOOTH
Sharing? It's our treasure! We don't need to share! We're pirates!

SQUID LIPS SID
We'd never share with you, you filthy seadogs.

CALICO JACK
Look, I know we're all pirates here and it's practically our jobs to fight over treasure, but this isn't just about the treasure any more. It's about our lives. It's about the king's pardon. I don't particularly like you, Squid Lips, but that doesn't mean I want you hanging.

SQUID LIPS SID
(*bares teeth*) You're too kind. Give us the treasure, then, if you feel so strongly about protecting my neck.

CALICO JACK
Hardly. I'm not a fool.

SHARK TOOTH
Well, /that

CALICO JACK
Shut up. Look, we'll open it together, and then we'll take it back to the king together, and we'll all get the pardon. Then you lot can do whatever you like.

SHARK TOOTH
Jack, I really /don't think

SQUID LIPS SID
(*vicious grin*) Sure. Sounds like a worthy plan to me.

SQUID LIPS SID and CALICO JACK shake hands, SLS trying to be intimidating and CJ ignoring his actions.

CALICO JACK
Right. Let's get this thing open.

The four PIRATES crowd around and open the box. They gasp and step back.

The SON in the box groans.

WHERE YOUR TREASURE IS

DECAYIN' DAVE
Squid Lips?

SQUID LIPS SID
What?

DECAYIN' DAVE
(*nervous*) Squid Lips, there's a man in our treasure box.

SHARK TOOTH
(*to CALICO JACK*) What kind of joke is this, do you think?

CALICO JACK
A bad one. Do you recognise the fellow?

SHARK TOOTH
He… reminds me of someone, but I can't put my finger on it.

CALICO JACK
(*beat*) It's the king's son.

Meanwhile DECAYIN' DAVE and SQUID LIPS SID help SON out of the box.

SQUID LIPS SID brushes SON down and straightens him up roughly while DECAYIN' DAVE hunts frantically in the box.

DECAYIN' DAVE
Squid Lips? Sid? (*surfaces*) Squid Lips, there's no treasure in here!

SQUID LIPS SID grunts.

DECAYIN' DAVE
No treasure! Nothing! Not a thing. (*dives into box again*)

SHARK TOOTH
Hear that, Calico? The plot thickens.

DECAYIN' DAVE
(*resurfacing*) Squid lips did you hear me? There's nothing here! Squid Lips, there's no treasure!

SQUID LIPS SID
Get out of the box, you idiot. Stop making a fool of yourself. Of course there's no treasure.

DECAYIN' DAVE
But... But... We were hunting treasure!

SQUID LIPS SID
Yeah, well, we got this, didn't we. (*shake SON roughly by the arm*)

SON winces but doesn't say anything. He is battered and exhausted.

DECAYIN' DAVE
But we can't trade him for drink!

SQUID LIPS SID
No, we can't. Useless, good-for-nothing... (*turns to CALICO JACK*). Is this your idea of a joke?

CALICO JACK
Hardly, Squid Lips. I was hunting the treasure too.

SQUID LIPS SID
You sure? 'Cause you're exactly the kind of fellow who'd lead us a merry dance just so's you could have free rein with the real treasure.

SHARK TOOTH
That's it, just come right out and say it, Squid Lips. No holding back, there. Don't keep it in, it's bad for your health.

SQUID LIPS SID
One of these days, Toothless, my fist will meet your head so hard you'll meet your maker.

SHARK TOOTH
Oo, scary. See me quiver.

SQUID LIPS SID
I can make it sooner rather than later, if you like.

SHARK TOOTH
Oh, sure, go right a/head

CALICO JACK
Look out!

SON collapses on the ground.

WHERE YOUR TREASURE IS

DECAYIN DAVE stares at him, helpless. CALICO JACK rushes to his side.

CALICO JACK
Get out of the way, Decayin' Dave. Look, here, let him breathe. Shark Tooth, water! The man's half dead, the sorry critter. (*gives him water to sip*) There, that's better, isn't it.

SON
(*Coughs and struggles to a sit*) Sorry.

CALICO JACK
Don't be sorry, sonny, it's not your fault.

SQUID LIPS SID
Ha! Likely story. Likely he ran away and got himself captured or some such, and now he's jolly near died for the effort. Serves him right.

SON
I... didn't run away.

SQUID LIPS SID
Yeah? Then what happened.

SON looks away in embarrassed silence.

CALICO JACK
Look, you just lie here for a bit until you feel better. We'll see about getting you some food, won't we Shark Tooth.

CALICO JACK drags SHARK TOOTH away to talk.

SHARK TOOTH
What are we going to do with him, Jack?

CALICO JACK
I don't know. This is confusing, strange. Why would the king send us to track down his son?

SHARK TOOTH
Perverse sense of humour?

CALICO JACK
You don't understand. His son's been missing for thirty-three years. Since he was born. He was born while the king was on a diplomatic tour, and the king came home without him.

SHARK TOOTH
He left his son behind?

CALICO JACK
I don't know! I mean, we thought so, but... I don't know.

SHARK TOOTH
So what do we do?

CALICO JACK
Well, we can't leave him with those idiots. (*sighs*) We'd better take him back to the king. (*goes to walk away*)

SHARK TOOTH
(*catches JACK'S arm*) What if it's a trap?

CALICO JACK
Then it's a trap I have to walk into. Find the treasure, find your heart. I've found the treasure, Shark Tooth. I need to find my heart.

CALICO JACK returns to the SON.

SHARK TOOTH watches him thoughtfully, then follows.

CALICO JACK
So, what are we going to do with the fellow, then, ay lads?

SQUID LIPS SID
I say we kill him.

SHARK TOOTH
(*rolls eyes*) You want to kill everything that moves.

SQUID LIPS SID
Oh yeah? I'll kill you, you worthless, no good—

DECAYIN' DAVE
(*holding SQUID LIPS back*) I've got a better idea.

SQUID LIPS SID
(*stops short*) You have an idea?

DECAYIN' DAVE
I do.

WHERE YOUR TREASURE IS

                         SQUID LIPS SID
Y' mean yer brain actually functions long enough to put a thought together?

                         DECAYIN' DAVE
What about we ransom him?

                         SQUID LIPS SID
Now that is an idea! Dave, I could almost say I was proud of you.

                         DECAYIN' DAVE
Aw, thanks, Squid Lips!

                         SQUID LIPS SID
Right, so, where do we stash him?

                         DECAYIN' DAVE
We could always put him back in the trunk...

                         SQUID LIPS SID
Dave, me hearty, you're on a roll! Let's put him /back in

                         CALICO JACK
Stop, Squid Lips. You're not doing anything with him.

                         SQUID LIPS SID
Oh yeah? Says who?

                         SHARK TOOTH
Says the rightful finders of the treasure, that's who.

                         SQUID LIPS SID
You have no proof you found him first.

                         CALICO JACK
Squid Lips, be reasonable. We all know we were here first.

                         SQUID LIPS SID
(*grins*) Dead men tell no tales, Jackie. And toothless sharks die young.

                         SHARK TOOTH
That's it! I'm sick of you lot! Thick as bilge water, you two. Get lost, before we have to beat you senseless!

SQUID LIPS SID
Like to see you try. We nearly had you before.

CALICO JACK
(*draws sword*) Then let's settle this, once and for all.

SQUID LIPS SID
No problem.

PIRATES yell and fight. CALICO JACK and SHARK TOOTH overcome SQUID LIPS SID and DECAYIN' DAVE and drive them off.

SHARK TOOTH
(*panting*) Well, that's the last of them for a while.

CALICO JACK
Don't be so sure. (*hauls SON to feet and support him*) Come on, then, lad. Let's get you home. Grab the map, Shark Tooth. No sense leaving that behind.

SHARK TOOTH
Aye, aye, Captain.

Exit all.

ACT IV

Scene 1

CALICO JACK and SHARK TOOTH study the map, with the SON tagging along behind.

SHARK TOOTH
Well, I'm glad we brought the map, but even so, I don't like the look of this place.

CALICO JACK
Valley of the Shadow of Death. Do you think...?

SHARK TOOTH
Look at the names of everything else on the map. They were true.

CALICO JACK
Yes, but... death?

WHERE YOUR TREASURE IS

SHARK TOOTH

Shadow of death. Not quite so bad, right? ...Right?

CALICO JACK

We have no other choice. There's no other way to get back to the castle short of going back around the way we came, and he won't make it that far. Not so bad. Right.

SHARK TOOTH

We could ditch the quest.

CALICO JACK

(*sigh*) Better to die on the road to treasure than by the hangman's rope.

SHARK TOOTH

Treasure? We were on the road to treasure. Now we're just on the road to take-the-king-back-his-son. I see no treasure on the horizon.

CALICO JACK

(*wearily*) Maybe the king will give us a reward.

SHARK TOOTH

Doubtful.

CALICO JACK

Then at least we'll have the reward of our lives! Or have you forgotten about the pardon? Come on, Shark Tooth. No sense prattling.

They walk onwards. The light fades as they walk.

SHARK TOOTH

Uh, Calico?

CALICO JACK

Yes, shark bait?

SHARK TOOTH

Does it seem darker to you?

CALICO JACK

Perhaps. But what have pirates to fear of the dark?

SHARK TOOTH

In the Valley of the Shadow of Death?

CALICO JACK pretends not to hear and they continue walking.

SHARK TOOTH
Um, Jack?

CALICO JACK
Mm?

SHARK TOOTH
It really is getting darker.

CALICO JACK
I know.

SHARK TOOTH
You don't... You don't think the map really means death, do you?

DECAYIN DAVE and SQUID LIPS SID bump into something offstage.

SHARK TOOTH
What was that?

CALICO JACK
I... Nothing. Nothing at all.

Another bump.

CALICO JACK and SHARK TOOTH stand back to back with swords drawn.

SON continues to trudge wearily onward, not noticing a thing.

CALICO JACK realises SON is leaving them behind.

CALICO JACK
Hey! Hey, you there. Wait! Hold up. You can't just go trudging off like that, you'll be killed.

SON
(*locks gazes with CALICO JACK*) I'm sorry.

CALICO JACK
It's fine, just... just stick with us, okay?

WHERE YOUR TREASURE IS

SON
(*shakes head*) You do not understand. You have found what you seek—others must find what they seek. I am sorry.

CALICO JACK
What? I mean... What?

SHARK TOOTH
Jack, look out!

SQUID LIPS SID and DECAYIN' DAVE burst onto the stage, swords drawn.

The pirates fight.

SQUID LIPS SID and D. DAVE have the advantage of surprise, and CALICO JACK is hard pressed to fend them off.

SHARK TOOTH is caught by surprise and nearly killed.

SON stepped in and takes the fatal blow, falling to the ground dead.

The pirates fight for a moment longer, during which CALICO JACK fatally injures SQUID LIPS SID, who staggers away to collapse stage left.

SHARK TOOTH
What have you done? No one can accept the king's offer now!

DECAYIN' DAVE
Us? Us? It... It was your fault!

CALICO JACK
Hardly, Dave. You attacked us.

DECAYIN' DAVE
I didn't attack you, I wouldn't attack you, I was coming to warn you, I was! Warn you before Squid Lips could attack!

SQUID LIPS SID
Decayin' Dave, if I could move you'd be a dead man!

DECAYIN' DAVE
No! No, I mean, I didn't, we didn't, honest, I promise... We didn't want trouble! All we wanted was the treasure! We didn't really want trouble...

DECAYIN' DAVE collapses into a heap front stage left.

SHARK TOOTH

Now that little episode is over. (*shakes head*) What are we going to do, Calico?

CALICO JACK

...Others must find what they seek.

SHARK TOOTH

What?

CALICO JACK

The son. He said that to me, right before they attacked. That we have what we were seeking, but that others must find what they sought.

SHARK TOOTH

Trouble.

CALICO JACK

Squid wanted trouble, and that's what he got.

SHARK TOOTH

(*beat*) So. What do we do now?

CALICO JACK

Take the body back, I suppose.

SHARK TOOTH

Are you insane? You're going to lug a dead body all the way back to the king's castle? What for?

CALICO JACK

It... seems like the right thing to do.

SHARK TOOTH

You're a pirate! You don't do the right thing by definition! It's a job requirement!

CALICO JACK

Perhaps. But pirate though I am, I still understand honour.

SHARK TOOTH

Honour? Honour! You've been off your ship too long, Calico. You're turning soft, like a landlubber.

WHERE YOUR TREASURE IS

CALICO JACK
Pirates live by the code, Shark Tooth. The code requires honour. Besides. We might still get the pardon. The proclamation never said the treasure had to be alive.

SHARK TOOTH
(*sighs*) You...

CALICO JACK
Yes?

SHARK TOOTH
Nothing. Here. Give me a hand. I'm not carrying this dead weight the whole way by myself.

CALICO JACK
Of course not, Shark Tooth. Of course not.

CALICO JACK and SHARK TOOTH exit, carrying the SON.

DECAYIN' DAVE
(*whimpering*) We're going to die! We're all going to die! We going to die and it's all your fault!

SQUID LIPS SID
Shut up, ye' blubbering whale! We just have to make the best of what's happened.

DECAYIN' DAVE
Best? Best? We're lost in the Valley of Death! We're going to die! I can't take this any more, I can't!

SQUID LIPS SID
Fine, don't. Get lost.

DECAYIN' DAVE
What?

SQUID LIPS SID
If ye can't take it, get lost. I don't want ye here.

DECAYIN' DAVE
Well... Well... Maybe I will!

SQUID LIPS SID
Go, already! Avast ye whingeing! Go and maybe I'll have some peace and quiet!

DECAYIN' DAVE

(*stands and backs away*) I... I... (*turns and flees*)

SQUID LIPS is left alone on the darkening stage.

SQUID LIPS SID

Dave? Decayin' Dave? Dave, get back here this intant! Ye'll not leave me to die alone! Get back here, scoundrel! Ratbag! No-good land-loving scallywag! (*beat*) Dave? Dave...

Lights fade.

ACT V

Scene 1

The king's chamber. The KING sits on his throne, attended by SERVANTS.

KING

Bring in the supplicants!

The SERVANTS usher in CALICO JACK and SHARK TOOTH, bearing the body of the SON.

KING

Welcome, pirates, to my castle. You have completed the quest, for which I commend you.

CALICO JACK and SHARK TOOTH put down the SON.

SHARK TOOTH

Yes. Well. About that...

CALICO JACK

We are sorry, King, but we have failed you.

KING

Why do you say that?

SHARK TOOTH

Not to put to fine a point on it, but... (*nudges the body*) he's dead.

CALICO JACK

He fought bravely, my lord, to the end, with true buccaneer spirit. We owe our lives to his courage.

WHERE YOUR TREASURE IS

SHARK TOOTH
(*aside*) And our broken backs to his considerable weight.

KING
(*gently*) Servants. Bring me my treasure.

The SERVANTS pick up the SON and carry him to a table.

The KING leaves his throne to stand over his SON. He touches the SON'S face tenderly and bows his head.

KING
Thank you. My treasure, my heart, the centre of my life, is restored. Servants! Bring in the pirates' reward!

SERVANTS enter bearing beautiful cloaks, small crowns and jewels.

They kneel before the PIRATES.

SHARK TOOTH
This... This is for us?

KING
You have completed my quest. You have upheld your part of the bargain, and passed safely through the trials I designed for you.

SHARK TOOTH
You designed those trials? Are you mad? Are you insane? We nearly died!

CALICO JACK
But we didn't. And we are very grateful for your rewards, king. Aren't we, Shark Tooth?

SHARK TOOTH
Oh. Yes. Very grateful. (*eyes the jewels*) Very grateful. But... what about the pardon?

CALICO JACK
Yes. Much as I do adore treasure, my lord, I adore my life rather more.

KING
And yet you nearly lost it. Why is that?

SHARK TOOTH
Because you designed traps for us, you big scallywag!

KING
(*amused*) But you didn't have to accept the quest, nor did you have to continue with it once you saw how hard it was. Plenty of other pirates gave up. And yet you continued to risk your lives. Why?

SHARK TOOTH
Because... Because... Because I follow my captain!

KING
Indeed. And your captain?

CALICO JACK
I... (*steels himself*) Because I would rather die questing than by a hangman's noose, sir.

KING
(*laughs*) Ah! Now that is a sentiment I applaud. But it begs the question for what have you spent your life questing?

SHARK TOOTH
Nothing. He just likes running around the countryside looking for things.

CALICO JACK
I... I am not sure I understand your question, sir.

KING
Oh, I think you understand me perfectly well, even if your friend here refuses to. You have spent your life in search of one thing or another. You have had treasure, you have had freedom, you have had everything man can desire. And yet still, you have spent your life questing. What is it you searched for?

CALICO JACK
I searched... For a reason, my lord. Treasure is all well and good—

SHARK TOOTH
And shiny.

CALICO JACK
And shiny. But it only serves a purpose after all. And freedom is of little use when one has no purpose for it. (*digs into pocket*) This, my lord, is what I sought. (*holds out compass*)

WHERE YOUR TREASURE IS

KING
Direction! (*claps*) Ah, very good. Very good indeed! Yes. I think that is what you sought. And it reflects well on you, Calico Jack—that is your name, is it not?—It reflects well on you that it is not that material end of your quest, but the journey, that you desire. Happiness, it has been said, is in the journey. (*thoughtful pause*) And yet, it occurs to me that you consider this quest incomplete.

CALICO JACK
I returned the treasure, sir, but not in... good condition.

KING
Then perhaps this shall reassure you.

KING goes to the body and bows over it. After several moments, during which SHARK TOOTH grows fidgety, the KING steps back.

KING
Behold, my power.

The SON wakes and sits.

SON
Father!

They embrace.

KING
Servants, take my son to his chambers. See that he is given clean clothing and is well fed.

The SERVANTS escort the SON away. After several lines, they return to take their places by the KING.

SHARK TOOTH
But... But... That's impossible!

KING
Impossible, or improbable?

SHARK TOOTH
Both! You can't bring people back from the dead! No one has that kind of power!

KING
(*mock surprise*) Really? (*looks at hands*) Well. I suppose we must all be hallucinating together then, mustn't we? (*waggles fingers*)

SHARK TOOTH
But... but... (*wails*) That's impossible!

CALICO JACK
Sir, if I hadn't seen it with my own eyes I'd say it was impossible. But as I saw it, I have to say instead that it's the sign of great power. So I must ask if you've had such power all along, why not use it against the pirates? Why are we still alive?

KING
Ah. Because with great power comes great responsibility, young Jack. I like to play by the rules.

SHARK TOOTH
But you could rule the entire world!

CALICO JACK
(*realisation dawning*) Because true power lies in not exercising it. (*beat*) I could respect a man who stood by his word.

KING
As could I.

CALICO JACK
(*beat*) Can you give me what I've been searching for? Can you give me a purpose greater than myself, something I can believe in and fight for?

KING
If you'll accept.

CALICO JACK
I... I think I'd like to accept, Sir.

KING
Very well. Servants, take the prince to his apartments!

CALICO JACK
(*looks around for the SON and starts as the servants approach him*) Me?

KING
If you'll accept.

CALICO JACK exits, dazed, with the SERVANTS.

WHERE YOUR TREASURE IS

                            SHARK TOOTH

(*beat*) Very clever.

                            KING

I beg your pardon?

                            SHARK TOOTH

Very clever. And technically, we're the ones begging your pardon.

                            KING

Witty fellow, aren't you. What is it that you find so particularly clever?

                            SHARK TOOTH

Your cunning little ploy.

                            KING

My ploy?

                            SHARK TOOTH

To get your son back.

                            KING

Was that the ploy, do you think?

                            SHARK TOOTH

I... Yes... No... Argh! You delight in vexing me. Why leave your son behind all those years ago if you had this kind of power? Why desert him?

                            KING

(gravely) For such a time as this, that I might have a way to show mercy upon those of mine enemies who chose to be worthy.

The KING gives SHARK TOOTH a significant look and SHARK TOOTH squirms.

                            KING

So. Does this mean that you will not accept my pardon?

                            SHARK TOOTH

Oh. Er, no. No, I think I'd like the pardon.

                            KING

Even though you see through my ploy?

SHARK TOOTH
Well... I mean, it wasn't really a ploy, was it. And the trials... They were only to test that we were strong enough, weren't they? So... You know.

KING
On balance, you'll accept.

SHARK TOOTH
Well... It's the logical thing to do, right?

KING
It's the logical thing to do.

SHARK TOOTH considers for a moment longer then exits.

The KING watches him, laughs, and exits also.

THE 5000

This story follows the story of the feeding of the five thousand from three different perspective: firstly a mother and daughter listening to Jesus speak; secondly two of Jesus' disciples wondering how on earth they will feed the masses; and finally the young boy who gave up his lunch, who must now explain to his mother why he didn't eat his food.

ACTORS REQUIRED

Male
3

Female
2

Either
1

MINIMUM TOTAL
6 or, with judicious costuming, 3

SCENE SUMMARIES

Scene 1

A mother explains to her hungry daughter that some things are more important than food.

Scene 2

Two disciples wonder how they will follow out Jesus' orders to find food for the massive crowd.

Scene 3

A young boy must explain to his mother that he gave his lunch away yet again, and try to convince her that being part of a miracle made it worthwhile.

CAST OF CHARACTERS

MUM
Woman in the crowd, listening to Jesus. Patient and focused.

CHILD
Young. Growing restless after sitting listening all day.

ANDREW
A disciple.

PHILLIP
A disciple.

MOTHER
Jewish mother. Somewhat concerned about social standing and proper behaviour.

BOY
Not afraid to sneak away to listen to Jesus. Awed to have been part of a miracle.

THE 5000

Scene 1

Two people sit on stage facing the audience. They are 'listening' to Jesus talk.

CHILD

Mum, I'm really hungry!

MUM

Hush, child, I'm listening.

CHILD

But Mum, I'm *hungry*!

MUM

He shouldn't be too much longer, dear. We can get some food after.

CHILD

But Mum, we haven't eaten since lunchtime! He's been talking for *ages*.

MUM

I know, dear. But I really want to hear what he has to say. I'm hungry too.

CHILD

Then can't we go eat?

MUM

No.

CHILD

But you said you're hungry.

MUM

(*looks directly at child*) I am hungry. But sometimes food isn't the most important thing.

CHILD
It *feels* like it is.

MUM
(*smiles*) I know. But your hunger will only last for a few hours.

CHILD
A few *hours*! That's forever! I can't be hungry for a few hours! I'll die!

MUM
I doubt that. But like I was saying, if you miss a meal, you can make up for it later. If we miss out on what Jesus is saying, we'll never get to hear it again.

CHILD
Couldn't someone, like, tell you what he said?

MUM
(*considers for a moment*) It's like this. Imagine I went for a picnic to the river and took all your favourite food, and went paddling afterwards. Would you prefer me to come home and tell you about it, or would you prefer me to take you with me?

CHILD
I'd want to go!

MUM
Well, there you go. I could get someone to tell me about what Jesus said, but nothing's the same as hearing it for myself.

CHILD
(*folds arms a bit sulkily*) Fine, then. We can listen. (*brightens*) But I want dessert tonight!

MUM
Do you just. Well, I'll see. Now be quiet.

Scene 2

Two of the disciples stand, listening to Jesus talk.

PHILLIP
It's getting late. Do you think he's going to finish up soon?

THE 5000

ANDREW
Not likely. He went on for quite a while down at Capernium.

Silence as Jesus continues to talk.

PHILLIP
(*gestures to the crowd*) People are getting restless.

ANDREW
Hungry, probably. I certainly am.

PHILLIP
Yeah, me too.

They listen some more.

ANDREW
Why'd you have to mention food? I really am hungry now.

PHILLIP
Me too.

More listening.

PHILLIP
Maybe we should go check on him. He does forget the time when he's talking sometimes...

ANDREW
Good idea. Off you go!

PHILLIP
What, me?! Why don't you go?

ANDREW
It was your idea. (*nudges PHILLIP*) Go on then.

PHILLIP sighs and exits. After a few moments he returns.

ANDREW
What did he say?

PHILLIP
(*disgruntled*) I asked him if he was going to send the crowd down into the town so they could get food and find accommodation for the night.

ANDREW
I know that; I want to know what he said?

PHILLIP
He told me to give the people something to eat.

ANDREW
What?!

PHILLIP
I know! Madness.

ANDREW
It would take eight months' wages to buy enough food for everyone! We can't afford that kind of money! We gave up paid employment when we decided to follow Jesus!

PHILLIP
I know. But what could I say? 'Ah, sorry Jesus, I don't want to spend all my money on food for these people; they'll have to go hungry.' I don't think so.

They shuffle a bit in silence.

ANDREW
So. What are we going to do?

PHILLIP
Dunno. I guess... I guess I could go ask him?

ANDREW
Yeah, ok, do that.

PHILLIP
I went last time! You could go.

ANDREW
You went before, so you're already in a conversation with him. Off you go.

Exit PHILLIP. ANDREW shuffles on stage, checking out the crowd. PHILLIP returns.

THE 5000

ANDREW
So, what'd he say this time?

PHILLIP
Asked me how many loaves we have.

ANDREW
What, us? None left! Surely he knew that!

PHILLIP
Yeah I know. What do we do now?

ANDREW
(*beat*) I guess we could ask the crowd...

Scene 3

Boy enters stage carrying an empty basket, followed by his mother who is in mid-rant.

MOTHER
...going off on your own like that, thoroughly irresponsible! After I specifically told you to stay with your brother! (*eyes basket*) Well, you're home safe, and at least you ate your lunch.

BOY
(*uncomfortable*) Uh, yes. About that.

MOTHER
(*suspicious*) What about it? *Don't* tell me you lost it. Well I'm not making you anything else. If you insist on losing the perfectly good lunch I made this morning, then that's your own fault and you can just wait till dinner.

BOY
(*interrupts, a bit desperate*) Mum! (*pauses to make sure she's actually listening*) I didn't lose it. I gave it away.

MOTHER
Oh son! Have those [NAME] twins been bullying you again? You really don't need to deal with them by yourself, you know. Did they threaten to hurt you if you didn't give them your lunch? Why those good for nothing little... Just wait till I see their mother!

BOY
Mum, no, that's not it!

MOTHER

Well, why did you give it away then?

BOY

(*mumbles*) Because he asked for it.

MOTHER

He? Who? Aw, did you meet a poor person who had no lunch? My son, giving his lunch away to the needy. What a wonderful child you are!

BOY

Uh, not quite. He wasn't exactly poor.

MOTHER

(*beams brighter*) A Pharisee! One of the Pharisees asked you for your lunch! Who was it? ...? ...? What an *honour*! Oh I'm so proud!

BOY

Mum, no! It was Jesus!

MOTHER

(*wary*) Jesus? That trouble-making fellow from Galilee? What were you doing near him?

BOY

I... Uh... Well, that's why... See, I didn't exactly run away from (brother). He wouldn't stay.

MOTHER

(*suspicious*) Wouldn't stay where?

BOY

(*mumbles*) To hear Jesus speak.

MOTHER

What? To... to hear him speak? You went to listen to him? I can't believe you! How many times have I told you to keep away from that man! Trouble follows him wherever he goes! You could have been kidnapped, or trampled, or killed! And you gave him your *lunch*! Forgot to bring some of his own, did he? (*shakes head*) Taking lunch from an innocent young boy! Of all the things!

BOY

Mum, no, it wasn't like that!

THE 5000

MOTHER
Well what was it like, then? Hmm?

BOY
We'd been there all day. Most people had eaten the food they had, and it was getting late. Everyone was hungry.

MOTHER
So Jesus stopped for a bite to eat, did he? Didn't consider maybe *ending his talk*, so everyone else could go home and eat.

BOY
Mum, no, let me finish! Everyone was hungry, and the disciples were going to go buy food.

MOTHER
(*surprised; she's curious now and forgets to be angry*) Buy food? For everyone? That would cost a fortune!

BOY
(*nods*) Uh huh. That's what Jesus said. And he asked if anyone had any food left over from lunch. (*shrugs*) No one else volunteered, and he looked hungry, so I gave him my left over fish and bread.

MOTHER
(*softens slightly*) Oh son. You are a good boy. You shouldn't have been hanging around him, but you are a generous lad.

BOY
But there's more. He took my bread, and prayed, and then told his disciples to pass the food out to everyone.

MOTHER
What, pass out your manky leftovers to the whole crowd? They must have got half a crumb each!

BOY
That's the amazing thing! There was plenty for everyone. And there was even some left over.

MOTHER
Sure. Your leftovers fed five thousand people. Okay then. Well, you've had a long day and must be tired…

BOY
Mum, it's true! Ask Gomer if you don't believe me! She was there too, she saw it all!

MOTHER
Really, Gomer was there?

BOY nods.

MOTHER
(*eyes boy thoughtfully*) You really went to see Jesus.

BOY nods.

MOTHER
And you shared your lunch.

BOY nods.

MOTHER
And Jesus prayed, and the food fed everyone.

BOY nods.

Silence, while they consider each other.

BOY
(*tentative*) Mum, isn't a miracle better than giving my lunch to a Pharisee?

MOTHER
A miracle? Well... I suppose...

BOY
It *was* a miracle, Mum. And I got to be part of it.

MOTHER
(*softens at last*) Oh son. (*hugs him*) You did well. You did very well.

GIFTS

A group of friends meet to discuss the gifts they got for Christmas. Three of them are unsatisfied one plans to return her gifts, another glumly considers hiding them in a drawer where he will never have to see them, and the third is so sure he will be disappointed by his gifts that he hasn't even opened them yet. A pair of angels arrive and point out to the teens (via a dreamlike vision) that they have a responsibility to use the gifts they have been given, and that they have been given them for a reason. The play concludes with the fourth friend, who comes from a wealthy background and often receives extravagant presents, revealing that she received the best present of all: a saviour.

ACTORS REQUIRED

Male
2

Female
2

Either
2

MINIMUM TOTAL
6

A Translation Note:
In Australia, where these plays were first written and performed, a jumper is the item of clothing known elsewhere as a sweater.

GIFTS

CAST OF CHARACTERS

BEN
Teenaged boy, risk adverse. Prefers the anticipation of an event to the event itself; lives in fear of disappointment.

ELMO
A polite, friendly teenaged boy who strives to do the right thing by others.

MOLLY
Preppy and smart teenaged girl, from a wealthy background.

SAMANTHA
A teen fashionista, up on all the current trends. Rather self-centred, though not maliciously.

ANGEL ONE
An angel, slightly senior to ANGEL TWO.

ANGEL TWO
An angel.

GIFTS

ACT I

Scene 1

A coffee shop. The four characters enter from the side, chatting as they come. They take seats at a table in the center of the room. BEN is carrying a backpack, in which is a wrapped present. ELMO is wearing a hideous jumper. MOLLY is well-dressed, with expensive but conservative clothing. SAMANTHA is a fashionista.

SAMANTHA
So did you all have good Christmases?

BEN
Yep.

MOLLY
Yeah, it /was great.

ELMO
Okay, I guess.

They reach the table.

SAMANTHA
Why only okay?

ELMO
(*taking a seat*) Well, I got this stupid jumper.

MOLLY
(*looks ELMO up and down*) What's wrong with it?

SAMANTHA
It's awful! I can't believe you're wearing it!

GIFTS

                             ELMO
(*looks miserable*) What can I do? My great aunt Bessie hand knitted it for me. I *have* to wear it.

                             BEN
Well, you don't *have* to. Not any more. You've worn it once, so she can be happy, and now you can stuff it in a drawer and say you lost it or something.

                             MOLLY
(*rolls eyes*) You lot are pathetic. Why can't you just be satisfied with the gifts you're given? I'll bet Great Aunt Bessie put a lot of effort into that jumper.

                             ELMO
Oh yeah. She put effort into making it as awful as possible, coz she knew I'd have to wear it!

SAMANTHA and BEN laugh.

                             ELMO
Anyway, what did you guys get?

Everyone looks at everyone else, wanting someone else to speak first.

                             ELMO
They weren't *that* bad, were they?

Silence.

                             ELMO
Oh come on, at least you guys don't have to *wear* them! Samantha?

                             SAMANTHA
Well, actually I *would* have to wear mine... But I'm not going to.

                             BEN
Why not?

                             SAMANTHA
I'm going to return it, just as soon as the shops open again.

                             MOLLY
I can't believe you. How can you just *return* a gift? Someone put a lot of thought and effort into buying them, and you just go and exchange them, like it doesn't matter!

BEN
Well, it doesn't, does it?

SAMANTHA
Yeah! Why *shouldn't* I exchange it for something I actually want? What's the point of keeping something I hate and will never use, just to make someone else happy?

MOLLY
(*throws up hands in disgust*) I despair of you all.

ELMO
Well what did you get then, Molly? A shiny new car? A trip to Europe?

MOLLY
(*blushing*) Look, just because my parents can afford nice stuff, doesn't mean I've never gotten a present I don't like.

BEN & ELMO
Oooo!

BEN
(*grinning*) Molly got something she didn't like too! What was it? A new ballgown? Personal hairdresser? (*sniggers*) Deportment lessons?

MOLLY
(*sticks tongue out at BEN*) Funny. But no. Anyway, at least I *opened* my present.

BEN goes quiet.

ELMO
Wait. You mean... Ben? You haven't *opened* your presents yet?

BEN looks miserable.

ELMO
Ha! You haven't opened them! Why on *earth* not?!

SAMANTHA
Yeah, why haven't you opened them? Christmas was a week ago!

BEN
(*mumbling*) Just didn't want to.

GIFTS

ELMO

You idiot! Why not?

BEN

(*louder*) Well, presents are fun, right? (*pulls some wrapped presents out of his backpacks and stacks them on the table. He stares at them*) It's exciting seeing them lurking around, wondering what's it them, knowing it's something new and exciting.

ELMO

(*plucks sleeve of jumper*) Might not be.

MOLLY

(*shooting a glare at ELMO*) But it might be, too. How would you know?

BEN

That's just it, though. At least this way, I can stretch the excitement out. Doesn't matter if I don't like it, because I don't know what it is.

MOLLY

Yes, but you can't *use* it!

BEN

Ah, but at least it will never wear out! *And* I don't have to exchange it!

MOLLY half stands then the four youths freeze as two angels enter the scene.

ANGEL ONE

So, what do you think?

ANGEL TWO

Yep. I'd say they need a lesson. Who do you want?

ANGEL ONE

(*gestures towards MOLLY and ELMO*) I'll take the two on the far side.

ANGEL TWO

That's right, you pick the easy ones.

ANGEL ONE

(*grins*) Oh well. Consider it good practice.

The angels stand one on either side of the table, ANGEL ONE behind MOLLY and ELMO and ANGEL TWO behind BEN and SAMANTHA.

ANGEL TWO reaches out and taps SAMANTHA on the shoulder.

ANGEL TWO
So, Samantha.

SAMANTHA turns to face the angel, but stares into the distance—throughout this section the YOUTHS respond to the angels, but are not consciously aware.

ANGEL TWO
You got some gifts recently.

SAMANTHA nods dreamily.

ANGEL TWO
And you're going to exchange them.

SAMANTHA nods again.

ANGEL TWO
What about the ones you can't exchange?

SAMANTHA tilts her head.

ANGEL TWO
You know, the ones you keep hiding? (*beat*) I'll bet the church could really use your graphics skills. The bulletin looks pretty dodgy, don't you think? And if they had some good posters maybe they could advertise that seminar better...

SAMANTHA bows her head.

ANGEL TWO
You can't exchange the gifts God's given you.

ANGEL ONE
(*taps ELMO on the shoulder*) Nice jumper.

ELMO hunches his shoulders.

ANGEL ONE
Looks warm though.

ELMO half shrugs.

ANGEL ONE
She didn't mean it to be horrible, you know.

GIFTS

ELMO shudders.

ANGEL ONE
Actually, she heard there was a mission trip to Peru towards the end of next year and thought it might keep you warm. (*beat*) It's done in a traditional Peruvian design, you know.

ELMO screws up his face.

ANGEL ONE
(*smiles wryly*) Yeah, another unwanted gift. You never *asked* to be good at street witnessing, I know. But you are.

ELMO sighs.

ANGEL ONE
But what are you going to do? Complain about it forever, wishing you could give it away? (*beat*) Or are you going to realise that it actually makes you kind of warm inside, and maybe it isn't so bad after all...

ANGEL TWO
(*to BEN*) So. You haven't opened your presents.

BEN idly nudges the presents on the table.

ANGEL TWO
Bet there are some cool things in there.

BEN stops playing with them.

ANGEL TWO
Ah. You're scared though. What if you don't like them? Or worse, what if you don't know how to use them?

BEN slumps. Meanwhile, ANGEL ONE crouches down and whispers inaudibly in MOLLY'S ear.

ANGEL TWO
(*gently*) But if you don't open them, you won't know. (*beat*) You know, you only missed the first one of those 'Finding Your Spiritual Gifts' seminars. I bet the pastor wouldn't mind if you joined in.

BEN hunches his shoulders.

ANGEL TWO
(*touches BEN on the shoulder*) You can't bury the gifts God gives you. Not without it killing you inside.

ANGEL ONE
(*standing*) You done? We need to be getting back.

ANGEL TWO nods.

ANGEL ONE
Let's go then.

The ANGELS exit.

MOLLY
(*sitting down, confused*) What was I saying?

SAMANTHA
(*looks at watch*) No idea, but I didn't realise it was so late. I have to get going!

MOLLY
Why, off to return your gifts?

SAMANTHA
Uh... maybe... not. I think... I think maybe they've grown on me. (*stands and gets ready to leave*)

MOLLY looks surprised.

BEN
(*looks at his watch*) What *is* the time? Whoa, it's that late already? I need to go too. (*swipes presents off table, puts them in backpack, and stands*) See you guys later.

ELMO
Let us know when you open those presents of yours!

BEN
(*shyly*) Uh, yeah, sure. Maybe when I get home. Anyway, see you!

SAMANTHA
Yeah, bye!

BEN and SAMANTHA exit. As they exit, ELMO speaks.

ELMO
(*pushing chair back*) We better get going too. You heading down Hayford Street?

MOLLY
(*nods and stands*) Let's go.

GIFTS

They tuck their chairs in.

MOLLY
So, what are you going to do with your jumper?

ELMO
(*shrugs*) Dunno. It's pretty warm. Might be useful if I ever went anywhere cold.

They head towards the exit.

ELMO
So, Molly, what *did* you get for Christmas?

MOLLY
(*smiles secretively*) The best gift of all.

ELMO
(*confused*) What?

MOLLY
Well, it's not exactly fashionable, and it's non-refundable, but it's satisfaction guaranteed... And it will last way beyond my lifetime.

ELMO
I don't get it. What did you get?

MOLLY
(*leads him towards the exit*) I got a Saviour.

TURNING POINT

King Manasseh lead Israel during a period of idolatry while the country was indentured to the Assyrian nation. While he is busy congratulating himself on the success of his international policies, culminating in the award of 'Most Favoured Nation' status, his advisers are plotting for better things—and God's prophet warns him of the consequences of ignoring God's decrees. Eventually, Manasseh is caught trying to cheat the Assyrians and the Assyrian king captures and tortures him. At last, all alone in the dungeon, Manasseh realises what the prophet had been trying to tell him all along about obeying God and repents. Restored once more to his kingdom, Manasseh mourns for his son Amon, who resents his father's newfound commitment to God. Nonetheless, Manasseh gathers together all of Israel's idols and burns them in a final act of deference to his God.

ACTORS REQUIRED

Male
10

Female
1

Either
2

MINIMUM TOTAL
8

SCENE SUMMARIES

ACT I: MANASSEH IS AWESOME—OR IS HE?

SCENE 1
Manasseh celebrates the fact that Assyria has awarded Judah 'Most Favoured Nation' status.

SCENE 2
Another party, but this time all might not be as wonderful as it seems.

ACT II: THE TURNING POINT

SCENE 1
Manasseh's methods are finally exposed for what they are: flawed. He is caught trying to cheat the Assyrian overlords and taken to Assyria.

SCENE 2
Manasseh is condemned to prison and torture by the Assyrian king, Esarhaddon.

SCENE 3
Manasseh tries desperately to justify his actions, but the words of the prophet ring in his ears, calling him to repentance.

ACT III: AND AFTER THAT

SCENE 1
Manasseh realises his poor decisions affect more than just himself, and laments for his 'lost' son Amon.

SCENE 2
Manasseh gathers together all the idols in preparation for burning, and realises that it isn't only physical things that can be idols.

SCENE 3

Manasseh burns the idols.

SCENE 4

In the modern world, a young girl asks her father about Manasseh, and learns the power of repentance.

CAST OF CHARACTERS

MANASSEH
King of Judah. He witnessed his father Hezekiah trying to live according to God's decrees, but Hezekiah also made some bad decisions that brought the kingdom to financial ruin. Manasseh has conflated the two in his mind, and thinks following God is stupid, illogical, and outdated. He has new, revolutionary ideas about developing an export trade for Judah (olives and olive oil), and is determined to implement his plans regardless of the cost to ensure peace and prosperity for his land.

PROPHET
A prophet of God, one of Manasseh's many counsellors. Extremely calm and collected, almost unmovable.

SOOTHSAYER
A fortune teller. Minor lines.

MEDIUM
A spiritist. Minor lines.

HADAD
A party-goer whose sister was murdered. One line.

ABIDAN
One of Manasseh's counsellors. He is aware of the growing gap between the rich and poor that is fueling civil discontent, and is not entirely on board with Manasseh's semi-secret plan to cheat the Assyrians out of their required tribute.

TURNING POINT

MELQART
One of Manasseh's counsellors. He is aware of the growing gap between the rich and poor that is fueling civil discontent, and is not entirely on board with Manasseh's semi-secret plan to cheat the Assyrians out of their required tribute.

MESTIPHALES
Counsellor to Manasseh. One line.

ESARHADDON
King of Assyria. A hard, harsh man—though he does have a pet kitten. Minor lines.

ASSYRIAN WARRIOR
Multiple required at various points. One line.

AMON
Manasseh's son. He was dedicated to Baal as a child and his life reflects this. Most notably, he is angry at his father for purging Judah of idols.

DAUGHTER
Young child in modern times who has been reading the story of Manasseh.

FATHER
Young child's father, who helps explain some of the effects of Manasseh's actions.

TURNING POINT

ACT I: MANASSEH IS AWESOME—OR IS HE?

Scene 1

The end of a party. The GUESTS are in the process of leaving, but the air is still one of celebration, and many of the GUESTS congratulate MANASSEH on their way out.

Once all the GUESTS are gone, MANASSEH returns and slouches over his chair, tired but happy. Note that he gave the order for Isaiah to be murdered, but is trying to hide this from everyone, including the PROPHET.

The PROPHET melts out of the shadows, almost as though he's been there the whole time (maybe he has). Throughout the play, the PROPHET is always super calm, controlled, collected, gentle but firm.

MANASSEH
A fabulous celebration, don't you think?

PROPHET
Of Isaiah's death?

MANASSEH
(*pretends to be startled*) Isaiah died?

PROPHET
'Murdered', I think, is not the same as 'died'.

MANASSEH
Oh. Well. These things happen, don't they?

PROPHET
Especially to those who disagree with you.

MANASSEH
What, are people still spreading those nasty rumours that I assassinate troublemakers? Who are they, I need to add their names to my list. (*beat*) No? Not even a little smile?

PROPHET
Lies are never funny.

MANASSEH
You mean the rumours, of course. I agree. Terrible things, lies. (*awkward silence*) But anyway, no. The celebration was over my special announcement. (*looks at PROPHET expectantly*) Oh come, you get everywhere. Surely you heard it? The Assyrians have granted us 'Most Favoured Nation' status!

PROPHET
Thrilling, I'm sure. Your father would roll in his grave.

MANASSEH
Oh, don't be ridiculous. You and I both know that trying to rebel against the Assyrians was the stupidest thing in a very long list of stupid that my father did. What did it get him? Thousands of people killed, the treasury completely emptied. Even the gold from his precious temple gone to pay the ransom. My father, sir, was an idiot.

PROPHET
Your father was only human, and all humans make mistakes. But he was a God-fearing man who did right by the law.

MANASSEH
Give it a rest, Prophet. You know my opinions there, and we've agreed to disagree.

PROPHET
No, sire, you agreed to disagree. I merely agreed that I would cease to harangue you about it at the time.

MANASSEH
Well you're haranguing now, so stop.

PROPHET
Sire, I really think you need to rethink your trade plans—

MANASSEH
My plans will make this nation the strongest it's ever been! Do you know what people are willing to pay for olives? This country needs stability, Prophet, and the only way to get that is to stabilise the economy.

PROPHET
The only way to achieve stability is to return to God.

TURNING POINT

MANASSEH
Enough! We are Assyria's favourite nation right now. The trade routes that will buy us are invaluable. I'm not tossing all that away to please some god who is jealous of other religions! Who are you to condemn those that choose a different way? If allowing my people to worship Asherah and Baal in the high places is what it takes to get peace, then that is what we will do!

PROPHET
Surely even your brand of peace does not involve sacrificing your son to foreign gods.

MANASSEH
(*a little shocked*) You know about that? Look, it was for show. I didn't mean it. Amon isn't even hurt; I passed him through the flames, it's not like I killed him. I'm not a heathen, despite what you think.

PROPHET
And yet you participate in their rites.

MANASSEH
Prophet, I am tired, and you are ruining my celebrations. You are dismissed.

PROPHET
(*hesitates*) It is never too late, my lord.

MANASSEH
Hmm? Too late for what?

PROPHET
Yahweh is always listening.

MANASSEH
Get out.

The PROPHET considers speaking, but changes his mind and exits.

MANASSEH is once again left draped over his chair, but this time the celebration is gone, and he is just tired.

Scene 2

Another party. People are still mid-chatter, though the party is coming to a close. There are two main groups centering around the SOOTHSAYER and the MEDIUM. ABIDAN and MELQART chat quietly off to one side. Their conversation is not heard by the others, and they are not listening to the others' conversations.

MANASSEH mingles with the crowd, energetic and happy. Occasionally he sends challenging glares at the PROPHET, who stands in the shadows to one side, watching with a blank expression.

SOOTHSAYER

(*choosing someone from the crowd*) And you! Don't do more of what isn't working for you. Tomorrow, do something unexpected, possibly even magical. Offer an olive branch.

After the FIRST PERSON nods, the SOOTHSAYER chooses another PERSON and considers them.

SOOTHSAYER

You... You would do well to be suspicious, I think. Careful. You know what I'm talking about.

The PERSON nods.

MEDIUM

(*eyes closed*) Sorry, what? Hada... Hadai... Hadad! Is there a Hadad in the room?

HADAD

That's me.

MEDIUM

Your ... aunt? No, sister. Your sister has a message for you. She says ... it was Mot who killed her.

The crowd around the MEDIUM gasp dramatically.

HADAD stalks angrily from the room.

ABIDAN

(*to MELQART*) I don't know. Did you hear about the riot?

MELQART

Yes. I know Manasseh tried to hush it up pretty quickly, but I have my sources.

ABIDAN

Me too. Only... they couldn't tell me who started it.

MELQART

Oh, it was one of the peasants. Someone complaining about Baruck's fountains again.

TURNING POINT

ABIDAN
It, ah, seems like there are more complaints than ever, lately.

MELQART
Indeed. But... sometimes... (*stage whisper*) one might almost think the peasants had it right, don't you think? The rich getting richer, the poor getting poorer?

MEDIUM
(*to a party-goer*) ...says be circumspect. Someone you think is your friend is actually your enemy.

ABIDAN
Oh, I'm not sure I'd go that far.

MELQART
No, no, of course not. I was just... repeating what someone else said to me the other day. Idiocy, of course. Pff. Peasants.

SOOTHSAYER
Oh, and dearie? Remember to trust your intuition. You see the situation more clearly than you allow yourself to believe.

ABIDAN
And yet, it's always worth keeping an eye out, know what I mean? I like... playing for the winning side.

MELQART
My kind of thinking. (*beat*) Assyria is still where the power is.

ABIDAN
We're small time compared to them.

MELQART
We need their support. Need to... pay our dues to them, to ensure their protection. (*stage whisper*) There's no way we could stand against Egypt or Babylon without them.

MEDIUM
Your mother would like to remind you that allies can be found in the most unlikely places, but she cautions you not to trust human logic.

ABIDAN
I know exactly what you mean. And I think that they, uh, would be happy for any assistance that ensured our ongoing servitude.

MELQART
Precisely. We are in agreement, then?

MELQART and ABIDAN nod, shake hands and exit, clearly in agreement, during the following exchange.

SOOTHSAYER
No, I'm sorry, that's all for tonight.

PARTY-GOERS protest.

SOOTHSAYER
Your Majesty, I'm flattered, but that really is all.

MANASSEH
Come, everyone. The party is over. Time for bed!

MEDIUM
Yes, even the spirits are tired, and we know what that takes.

PARTY-GOERS laugh and exit.

MANASSEH shakes hands with the SOOTHSAYER and the MEDIUM and thanks them for their time and attendance, then they too exit.

MANASSEH drapes himself over his chair, happy but tired.

PROPHET
(*appearing from the shadows*) Happy with yourself, are you?

MANASSEH
Why do you always appear to ruin special occasions? I'm reasonably sure your job description does not include the phrase 'party-pooper'.

PROPHET
(*a little tartly*) Given I answer to God for my 'job description', I highly doubt that you have any idea what it involves.

MANASSEH
Prophet? Don't test me. Not tonight.

PROPHET
Or what? You'll kill me, like Isaiah?

TURNING POINT

MANASSEH
That was ten years ago, man, and you're still on at me about it?

PROPHET
The Lord does not forget.

MANASSEH
Yeah, well, maybe he should once in a while. No wonder he's so cranky. The guy needs to chill out a little.

PROPHET
(*furious, the only time he is not super-calm, though he is still tightly controlled*) You will not speak about Yahweh in such terms.

MANASSEH
Hey, you do have emotions after all. I was starting to wonder.

PROPHET
Is it not enough that you have turned the Lord's high places into temples for idols? Is it not enough that you have forsaken his path to forge your own in your arrogance and pride? Is it not enough that you have forced your people into servitude to the Assyrians, that your precious 'export trade' has turned half the nation against the other, rich against poor, wealthy against destitute, haves against havenots? Now you will blaspheme the Lord God Almighty as well? Mark my words, sir the day will come when you will regret your decisions, and it is coming sooner than you think.

MANASSEH
And what's that supposed to mean?

PROPHET
Just what I said: the Lord is warning you, Manasseh. Reconsider your ways, or they will be your ways no longer. Call upon the Lord, or he will call down his judgment and shower his wrath upon you. Turn from your pride before it brings you and all you hold dear to ruin.

MANASSEH
Get out.

PROPHET
Sire—

MANASSEH
OUT! Before I have you killed for your cheek. Get out of my sight, and don't venture into it again.

PROPHET exits.

MANASSEH
Of all the... Ways turn to ruin. Wrath and judgment! Ha! My reign has been the most stable period in the entire history of Judah. (*shouts at the door*) Do you hear that? In the entire history! Whatever. It was about time I fired him anyway.

ACT II: THE TURNING POINT

Scene 1

The court of King Manasseh.

Manasseh's COUNSELLORS, including MESTIPHALES, ABIDAN and MELQART, surround the throne. ASSYRIAN WARRIORS hide strategically around the stage/audience.

MANASSEH enters with the PROPHET trying to stop him.

PROPHET
The hour is near, my king. I beg you, look to the Lord!

MANASSEH
Guards! Guards? Prophet, get out of my sight before I have you killed.

PROPHET
The hour of his judgment is at hand! Repent!

MANASSEH shakes the PROPHET off.

The PROPHET considers trying to go after him one last time, but gives up and leaves despondently.

MANASSEH approaches his COUNSELLORS exuberantly, taking his throne as he speaks.

MANASSEH
Well, my trusty advisors, it seems that things have worked out very well indeed. Trade is up two hundred percent, losses are down, and we haven't had a riot in weeks.

ABIDAN
(*muttering to MELQART*) Yes, a string of public hangings will do that.

MELQART stifles a snort.

MANASSEH
What was that?

TURNING POINT

MELQART
Uh, nothing, my lord. We were just... admiring your Majesty's crowd control policy.

MANASSEH
Indeed. Please continue admiring it, lest you end up falling prey to it.

MELQART stiffens at the threat and nods. This time it is ABIDAN who stifles a snort.

MANASSEH
And best of all, it seems that our little counterfeit has escaped the notice of the Assyrians.

ABIDAN
(*feigning ignorance*) Oh? Was that at the meeting I missed?

MANASSEH
(*very happy to have another excuse to detail his 'wonderful' plan*) Oh! We've almost completely gotten rid of our tributes to Assyria! I decided the tribute was eating into our profit margin too much. But of course, we couldn't just stop outright or the Assyrians would notice and come down on us like thirty talents of gold. So, Mestiphales here (*he claps MESTIPHALES on the back*) devised a—what was it?

MESTIPHALES
Graduated tribute reduction scheme.

MANASSEH
That's right, a graduated tribute reduction scheme. And it worked! Last month, we sent exactly NOTHING to the Assyrians!

MELQART
Aren't you afraid there might be repercussions?

MANASSEH
If the Assyrians were watching us that closely, they would have done something before now. Most Favoured Nation, remember? They would never suspect that we'd do something like this.

ABIDAN
(*quietly, signalling behind his back*) Oh, I think maybe they just might.

The ASSYRIAN WARRIORS leap into action at ABIDAN'S signal.

MANASSEH
What treachery is this?!

ABIDAN and MELQART alone are not seized by the ASSYRIANS.

ABIDAN
Ah, well, my lord. You win some and you lose some, isn't that what you always used to say?

MELQART
(*as the ASSYRIAN WARRIORS drag MANASSEH off*) Farewell! It's been lovely knowing you! Send us letters from prison.

ABIDAN
If they let you keep your hands.

MELQART sniggers. The last of the COUNSELLORS is carted away by the ASSYRIANS.

MELQART
Ah, well. That was fun.

ABIDAN
Indeed. (*beat*) Race you to the throne?

ABIDAN and MELQART race for the throne and fight good-naturedly over it.

Scene 2

King ESARHADDON of Assyria sits on his throat with Ninip, his pet cat.

MANASSEH stands before ESARHADDON in chains, with a ring through his lip. Attached to this is a chain or rope, by which an ASSYRIAN WARRIOR is restraining him.

MANASSEH is obviously injured and in pain.

ESARHADDON
So, you thought you could defy your rulers, did you?

When MANASSEH doesn't answer, the ASSYRIAN WARRIOR tugs on the lead, obviously hurting his lip.

MANASSEH
No! No, I never meant...

ESARHADDON
Enough. I know exactly what it was that you were attempting to do. I have affadavits here (*waves them*) signed by members of your own council. Guard?

TURNING POINT

ASSYRIAN WARRIOR

Yes, sire.

The ASSYRIAN WARRIOR escorts MANASSEH offstage and beats him. MANASSEH screams and cries out, etc.

ESARHADDON

Stop. Bring him here.

The ASSYRIAN WARRIOR returns with MANASSEH, who looks considerably worse for wear.

MANASSEH

My lord, I am sorry, I—

ESARHADDON

Shut up. I do not wish to hear your grovelling. I know what you have done, you know what you have done, and you will be kept in the prison for the amusement of my soldiers until I decide what to do with you. (*To the GUARD*) Take him away. Tell your men they may do what they like with him, only keep him alive until I make my decision.

The ASSYRIAN WARRIOR nods and takes MANASSEH offstage again.

ESARHADDON

Vassals. You think you have all your slave states in a row, and then one of them goes and pulls a stupid stunt like this. What is the world coming to, Ninip?

Scene 3

MANASSEH lies asleep in the prison cell, tossing and turning. He remembers the words of the Prophet in a dream.

PROPHET can be offstage, and deliver his lines via voice over, or could appear onstage in MANASSEH'S dream, disappearing when MANASSEH wakes.

MANASSEH

(*dreaming*) What have I done?

PROPHET

...you have forsaken His path in order to forge your own...

MANASSEH

I was just trying to avoid the mistakes my father made! I wanted to be a good king! I was trying to make Judah a better place. And I did! Judah is the wealthiest it's ever been, people are happy, the nation is stable, and I did that, me, I did it!

PROPHET
...turned half the nation against the other, rich against poor, wealthy against destitute...

MANASSEH
I didn't turn anyone against anyone! I was promoting peace! Harmony! Why do you think I allowed the other religions in the first place?

PROPHET
...you have turned the Lord's high places into temples for idols...

MANASSEH
No! I didn't... I mean, I had to! They wouldn't let me go ahead with my export plans if I didn't. My counselors, they didn't trust me, didn't trust my plan. It was the only way to keep them happy!

PROPHET
...the day will come when you will regret your decisions...

MANASSEH
I don't. Not at all. I did what I needed to do, and the country was happy, prosperous. People loved me.

PROPHET
...you will blaspheme the Lord God Almighty...?

MANASSEH
What does it matter? What could Yahweh possibly have for me? My father followed Yahweh, and look where it got him. The country was ruined. Destroyed!

PROPHET
...he was only human... all humans make mistakes...

MANASSEH
I... I am only human. (*beat*) But it was for a good cause! I meant well!

PROPHET
...the only way to achieve stability it to return to God...

MANASSEH
Return to God. Return to God! How can I return to God? Even if I wanted to, the Prophet said it himself: God never forgets. Even if—and I'm only saying IF—Yahweh was the right path to take, even IF I screwed everything up by walking my own way, what does that matter now? God doesn't forget, and I... I am broken.

TURNING POINT

PROPHET

...call upon the Lord... repent...

MANASSEH

Repent. My father taught me that word, when I was six. Repent means to be truly sorry for what you've done, he said. (*beat*) He was a good man, my father. A... a God-fearing man. (*beat*) And God saved him, I'd almost forgotten that. He was supposed to die, but he prayed, and God heard him, and he lived. (*trying hard to remember*) There... there was a sign. That's right, the sun! God moved the sun backwards as proof that he would save my father. I'd forgotten about that. (*beat*) Of course, my father spent his whole life trying to please God. He was the kind of person God would listen to. God wouldn't listen to me.

PROPHET

...Yahweh is always listening... It is never too late...

MANASSEH

Never too late. Always listening.

MANASSEH wakes and looks around for the PROPHET, who is not there.

MANASSEH

Huh. (*beat*) Oh. (*beat*) Um. (*beat*) ...Yahweh? Can... you hear me? (*beat, then he sighs and scrambles to his knees*) I think this was how my father used to do it. Now, how did he start, again? (*mumbles to himself, lips moving as he tries to remember*) Right. Ahem.

O Lord, Almighty God of our fathers Abraham, Isaac, and Jacob, God who made heaven and earth, who bound the seas, who shut up the deep, and before whom all men tremble, er... hi. Word has it that you in your great goodness have promised repentance and forgiveness to those who have sinned against you, that they might be saved.

That's... that's me, God. I'm a sinner, so you have in your justness granted repentance and forgiveness to me, and I'm here to claim them.

My sins are pretty huge, Lord, huge enough that I am not worthy to see even a glimpse of your heaven. I provoked you with my every action, thinking I could do things my way, that your way was faulty and my decrees were better than yours. I set up abominations in your holy places. I'm ashamed, God. I'm ashamed of what I've done, and I beg you to forgive me, not to let my sins destroy me.

Please, don't be angry with me forever, because you are the God of those who repent. I know this is true, and because you are good I know you will save me, even though I am unworthy, because it will show your mercy.

...Um, how do I end? Oh, right. Therefore I will praise you for all the days of my life, for all the powers of heaven praise you, and yours is the glory forever and ever, amen.

Scene 4

MANASSEH is back in his kingdom and ready to do God's will, though he still bears marks from his imprisonment. Together with the PROPHET and some of his COUNSELLORS (notably ABIDAN and MELQART, who are of course miserable that he has returned), he is surveying the kingdom to see where to start.

MANASSEH

Ah, it's good to be back!

ABIDAN

Yes, sire. It's, uh, good to have you back. (*to MELQART*) Isn't it?

MELQART

Oh, yes. Very good. Very-very... good.

MANASSEH

(*ignoring them*) So, Prophet. Where do you suggest I begin?

PROPHET

Well, sire, I think the houses of worship should be your first port of call. Especially the temple.

MANASSEH

Excellent, excellent. Yes, indeed. Worship it is. Nothing else runs straight if God's not in the house, isn't that right?

MELQART

Yes, sire.

ABIDAN

Indeed.

MANASSEH

Right, well, I think it's time. Come, I'm feeling generous. You can all stand with me while I address the people.

MANASSEH climbs a podium and addresses the crowd.

MANASSEH

People of Judah! People of Judah, the kingdom of God is at hand! For years, now, I have sought to unite us under one leadership, one goal, one king. My goals were admirable, but I had made one fatal flaw: I had decided that the king under which we should be united was me. How foolish I was! But Yahweh, in his ever-living grace and mercy, has granted me a second chance. Join with me, people, as we (CONTINUED)

TURNING POINT

strive to rebuild our kingdom, rich with poor, slave with master, under the leadership of the one true king: our God, the only God, Yahweh Almighty! We must begin by removing the idols from within our walls, cleansing the high places and consecrating them one more unto God. And so I task you now: go out, cleanse your homes, cleanse your workplaces, and dedicate all that you have to God!

ACT III: AND AFTER THAT

Scene 1

MANASSEH is in his throne room, pacing. He alternates between happy and enthusiastic as he remembers God, and despondent as he remembers what he is losing.

The PROPHET enters.

MANASSEH
How is the clean up going?

PROPHET
Well enough.

MANASSEH
But?

PROPHET
People are... used to the way things are. They're... resisting change.

MANASSEH
It's the temple, isn't it. I knew that would be the major problem.

PROPHET
They've been worshipping Baal and Asherah there for decades. Your sudden reversal of your decision makes no sense to them.

MANASSEH
Prophet, I'm not even sure it makes sense to ME. I just know that God spoke to me in that cell, just as He's been speaking to me through your words all my life.

PROPHET
The ways of Yahweh are often mysterious to man.

MANASSEH
Ha, you got that right. (*beat*) I really thought the export trade was the way to go, you know? It was such a clever idea.

PROPHET

It was.

MANASSEH

And it worked, for a while.

PROPHET

It did.

MANASSEH

(*frustrated*) It was all such a waste, you know? Everything I worked for, everything I tried to do. It worked for a while, but it made things worse in the end, didn't it? I mean, the country was a bit of a mess before, but at least we were all in the SAME mess, you know? None of this upper and lower class divide, Jews fighting Jews, the nation fragmented.

AMON knocks at the door.

MANASSEH

Amon, my son! Come in! What can I do for you?

AMON

This has to stop.

MANASSEH

What does?

AMON

This... (*waves his hand outside*) Whatever madness it is that has inspired this ridiculous turn of events.

MANASSEH

But son, it's not ridiculous. I've been doing everything wrong, God showed me that, and now I want to try to make things right.

AMON

Right? Right for whom? I grew up with those Asherah poles your guards are destroying.

MANASSEH

But son, Yahweh says—

AMON

Yahweh? That's who this is about? That ridiculous god your father worshipped?

TURNING POINT

MANASSEH
He's not ridiculous, He—

AMON
Save it, father. You think one discussion can challenge everything you've ever taught me? I know all about Yahweh, and your father and his stupidity, and I want none of it. Let me keep the poles.

MANASSEH
So that's what this is about.

AMON
Yes.

MANASSEH
(*beat, then he sighs*) I'm afraid I can't let you do that, son.

AMON
One set. One set of poles is all I'm asking for, for my own private worship.

MANASSEH
No. I have told the people that I will not tolerate the worship of Asherah or Baal anywhere in Judah. What kind of a man would I be if I made an exception in my own family?

AMON
A good father, that's what!

MANASSEH
I'm sorry, son. They have to go.

AMON
(*to the PROPHET*) This is all your fault!

AMON storms from the room.

MANASSEH
This is worth it. Please tell me this is worth it.

PROPHET
It is difficult, I know, but yes, it is worth it.

MANASSEH
It's just... my own son, you know? I had hoped he would support my decision, come to know Yahweh himself.

PROPHET

You dedicated him to Baal. What did you expect?

MANASSEH

I don't know. You're right. Not only have I wasted my life, I've wasted his, too. And now he's lost forever.

PROPHET

You do not know that.

MANASSEH

I fear I do. I at least had the memory of my father to ground my relationship with Yahweh. Amon has nothing. All his memories are of a father who caved to public pressure in order to try to make a name for himself. (*beat*) I've wasted it all, Prophet.

PROPHET

But God can restore it.

MANASSEH

I don't see how.

PROPHET

No. Neither can I at this moment. But I have faith. God will uphold you. Have faith.

Scene 2

A courtyard. Various SERVANTS come in and out, piling things on the floor—the idols and so forth that have been stripped from the places of worship.

MANASSEH and the PROPHET oversee the collection.

MANASSEH

...And we really have to burn all this?

PROPHET

No. That was your idea. But if you don't, you have to ask yourself: will you be tempted to pick it all up again? To allow it in?

MANASSEH

I suppose you're right. Better to get rid of it for good.

PROPHET

That's right. Be strong once, and you'll never have to worry about it again. If you're weak now and let it linger around, you'll have to be strong every time you see it.

TURNING POINT

MANASSEH
I know. It's just... harder than I thought.

PROPHET
God never promised that following him would be easy.

MANASSEH
Too right.

A SERVANT enters, bearing some item that MANASSEH was particularly attached to.

MANASSEH
Oh! Not that, too!

PROPHET
It all has to go, sire. God must come first if you are to have the life you desire.

MANASSEH
(*despondent*) It better be as good as you say it will be.

PROPHET
Not as good as *I* say it will be; as good as *God* says it will be. And he does not go back on his word.

MANASSEH
(*beat*) And yet I have to.

PROPHET
Mmm?

MANASSEH
Go back on my word. I told the people to do this. It's my fault. I encouraged them.

PROPHET
True. But you cannot let your guilt become an idol either.

MANASSEH
What do you mean?

PROPHET
An idol is very simple: at its core, it is merely anything that comes between us and God.

MANASSEH
Oh. That could be lots of things.

PROPHET
Indeed. It is difficult to keep our relationship right with God.

MANASSEH
Then why does he have to make it so difficult?

PROPHET
He doesn't. It is easy. All we have to do is come to him.

MANASSEH
Just... come?

PROPHET
Yes. But that is the hard part, of course. So many things in our lives can distract us from coming to God. Other gods, other religions, but also, for example, our guilt.

MANASSEH
Oh. Yes. (*beat*) What can I do about it, though? I feel guilty. I did things wrong. I *should* feel guilty!

PROPHET
Of course. And that is right; to repent you must regret what you have done. But it is only repentance if it leads you to God; if your guilt grows into a burden that prevents you from finding God, then it is not repentance, but an idol.

MANASSEH
Heavy stuff.

PROPHET
Guilt can be a heavy burden to bear.

MANASSEH
It can. It is. (*beat*) I don't know how to bear it.

PROPHET
Take it to God, along with your idols. Let your guilt burn in the fire, along with everything else.

MANASSEH
You know, that sounds like a great idea. I might do that. Thanks.

TURNING POINT

Scene 3

A bonfire. The PROPHET and MANASSEH stand nearby, ready to throw the idols into the flames.

PROPHET

Are you ready?

MANASSEH

I am.

PROPHET

Then go! Let all your idols go, and pray to God that he will remove the stumbling blocks from your life.

MANASSEH

(*flinging items into the fire*) Thank you, God, for your forgiveness! Accept the worthless rubbish of my old life so that I will carry it no more. Cleanse my life with this fire, and make me new. Amen.

Scene 4

Modern times. A FATHER is sitting alone reading when his young DAUGHTER runs up.

DAUGHTER

Daddy, Daddy! Guess who we learned about at church today?

FATHER

Who's that?

DAUGHTER

King Maness, Nanass, Manasseh!

FATHER

Oh? And who is he?

DAUGHTER

He was the king of Judah. He was a bad king, but then he repented, so he was a good king. (*beat*) Daddy, what does 'repented' mean?

FATHER

It means that he was very sorry for what he had done.

DAUGHTER
Oh. (*beat*) But why did that make him a good king? He still did bad stuff.

FATHER
He did. But when we repent, God forgives us for doing bad things. It says in the Bible that he will blot out our wrong-doing, and love us like it never happened.

DAUGHTER
Is that like last week, when I smacked Jon the arm, and you asked me if I was sorry, and I said I was, so you said that it would be okay?

FATHER
Yes, just like that.

DAUGHTER
(*beat*) But Jessie still won't talk to me.

FATHER
(*hugs her*) Yes, sometimes the wrong things we do have consequences that we have to deal with.

DAUGHTER
What were the conse, conque—

FATHER
Consequences?

DAUGHTER
Yes, those. What were they for King Manasseh?

FATHER
Well, there isn't much in the Bible about it, but it does say one thing: Manasseh had a son, Amon, and he grew up to be a very bad person. I think that was a consequence of Manasseh's actions, because when his son Amon was small, Manasseh set a bad example for him. Even when he repented and God forgave him, he couldn't erase the bad influence he had been on his son.

DAUGHTER
Oh. That's sad. It would be sad to have a bad son, wouldn't it?

FATHER
It would.

TURNING POINT

DAUGHTER
But Manasseh wasn't a bad king?

FATHER
He started out a bad king, but we don't remember him like that, that's right. We remember him because he showed how wonderful repentance can be.

FATHER continues reading.

DAUGHTER
Dad?

FATHER
Mmm?

DAUGHTER
What if Amon repented? Would he be a good son then?

FATHER
Yes. He would be a very good son.

DAUGHTER
Oh. (*beat*) In that case, I repent of breaking your fishing rod. See? Now I'm a good daughter.

DAUGHTER skips off.

FATHER stares after her, shocked, then as he processes what she said, he smiles and laughs. He collects up his things and exits after her.

IN SEARCH OF FREEDOM

A group of Israeli teens are left behind when Moses leads the rest of the Israelite nation out of Egypt. As they try their best to catch up with the main group, they come across some interesting characters that make them reconsider what freedom really means. Hepzibah, an old Israeli woman, is refusing to leave with the Exodus because she believes God wouldn't have had her born into slavery if He didn't mean for her to continue in it; shallow Egyptian woman Jamila and Nefertari realise that they are incapable of caring for themselves now that their slaves are gone; and Egyptian teen Hathor surprises the Israeli teens by asking to join them on the quest, seeking to know more about their God. Sadly, it seems that not all of the Israeli teens have what it will take to find their families and experience God's plan for freedom in their lives.

ACTORS REQUIRED

Male: 3

Female: 7

Either: 0

MINIMUM TOTAL: 8

IN SEARCH OF FREEDOM

SCENE SUMMARIES

Act 1

SCENE 1
Belial and Daniel wake Hannah up with the news that the Israelites have been released and are leaving Egypt.

SCENE 2
Belial, Daniel and Hannah meet up with Gomer, Ehud and Sarai and set out in pursuit of the Israelites.

SCENE 3
Realising that they have been left behind, the group set off to catch up. They meet an old Israeli woman who has refused to leave because she was born a slave, and Belial decides that he'd rather try to find his own way through town than follow the needs of the group.

Act 2

SCENE 1
Nefertari and Jamila realise the implications of their slaves departing—they are unable to care for themselves in the luxurious manner they are used to. They attempt to misdirect the Israeli teens, but the teens carry on successfully and encounter Hathor, an Egyptian teen who bargains directions for the chance to come with them and know their God.

Act 3

SCENE 1
The teens meet up with Belial on the far edge of town and witness the crossing of the Red Sea. Ehud, Gomer, Sarai and Hathor determine that they will take the long way around and catch up with the Israelites in the desert, but Belial, Daniel and Hannah decide that they would rather not risk their lives for freedom, and return to the city.

CAST OF CHARACTERS

HANNAH
A teenaged Israeli girl. Rather vague and silly.

DANIEL
A teenaged Israeli boy. Rather straightforward in character.

BELIAL
A teenaged Israeli boy. Easily discouraged. Prefers the obvious, logical option.

GOMER
A teenaged Israeli girl. Somewhat bossy.

EHUD
A teenaged Israeli boy. A natural leader who pulls the group together—usually.

SARAI
A teenaged Israeli girl. Sweet and kind; sensitive to the needs of others.

HEPZIBAH
A cranky old Iraeli woman who is very set in her ways.

NEFERTARI
A somewhat shallow Egyptian woman, friends with Jamila.

JAMILA
A somewhat shallow Egyptian woman, friends with Nefertari.

HATHOR
An Egyptian girl intrigued by the Israelite people; wants to know more about their God.

IN SEARCH OF FREEDOM

ACT I

Scene 1

It is the night after the first Passover in Egypt. The Israelites have just been informed that they may leave Egypt.

HANNAH's room. HANNAH lies sound asleep on her bed, snoring loudly.

DANIEL

(*offstage*) Hannah! Han-nah!

Hammering at door.

BELIAL

Eww, watch where you're hammering. The blood is still sticky on the doorpost.

DANIEL

Oh gross, it's all over my hand!

BELIAL

Hey! What are you doing! Don't wipe that on me! You're feral.

DANIEL

Well you have a turn then.

BELIAL

Hey Hannah, are you in there? Open up!

More hammering. HANNAH sleeps through it all.

DANIEL

Maybe she left already?

BELIAL

I didn't see her in the square though...

IN SEARCH OF FREEDOM

Hammering at door.

DANIEL
Hannah! We know you're in there!

BELIAL
Open up!

HANNAH wakes up slowly, yawns and stretches.

DANIEL
HANNAH!!

HANNAH
All right, all right, I'm coming!

HANNAH opens the door. Enter DANIEL and BELIAL.

BELIAL
What on earth have you been doing?

HANNAH
(*confused*) Uh, I was sleeping. Isn't that what most people do during the night?

DANIEL and BELIAL exchange exasperated looks.

DANIEL
She doesn't know.

HANNAH
Doesn't know what? What don't I know?

BELIAL
You mean you really slept through all that?

HANNAH
Slept through what? What's going on?

BELIAL
I can't believe you slept through the noise!

DANIEL
Are you sure you're all right? You're not sick or anything?

HANNAH

(*now extremely impatient*) What are you talking about? What is going on?

DANIEL

We're leaving.

HANNAH

You just got here!

DANIEL

Not us, the Israelites. We're leaving. Pharaoh's decided to let us go. Moses has been assembling the people since before sunrise. We're leaving any minute now.

HANNAH

What?

BELIAL

(*grabs HANNAH by the wrist*) Oh for crying out loud, come *on*. We're late already.

HANNAH

But I need to pack my things!

DANIEL

Don't worry about that. The Egyptians are donating a whole heap of stuff. They're scared that if we stay any longer they'll *all* die.

HANNAH

But my—

BELIAL

Come *on*! (*Drags HANNAH off*)

Exit BELIAL, HANNAH and DANIEL, stage right.

Scene 2

Enter GOMER, EHUD and SARAI from stage left. They are waiting in an outdoor area for their three friends to arrive.

SARAI

I really hope the others hurry up. Moses will be leaving any second now.

IN SEARCH OF FREEDOM

EHUD
Calm down, Sarai, it's all going to be fine. They'll turn up.

GOMER
It's typical, though, isn't it. I bet it was Hannah, she's *always* late, for everything!

SARAI
Gomer! You don't know it's her fault.

GOMER
(*shrugs*) Well, *is* always late.

EHUD
Listen, I hear something.

DANIEL
(*offstage*) Come *on* Hannah! Hurry up!

GOMER
(*to SARAI*) See. I told you it was Hannah's fault.

DANIEL and BELIAL run onstage from left, dragging HANNAH with them.

DANIEL
Hey. We're here.

BELIAL
(*glances at HANNAH*) Finally.

EHUD
Never mind all that, we need to get going. The Israelites are all meeting in the fountain square and I don't think Moses was planning to hang around for long.

Exit ALL, offstage right.

Scene 3

The fountain square. Trumpets sound.

The ISRAELITES run on stage from left, panting. HEPZIBAH is sitting, silent and motionless, down stage left. The ISRAELITES don't see her.

EHUD
Ok, this is where they were supposed to meet.

They look around.

SARAI
Uh? Where is everyone?

HANNAH
Maybe God made them invisible, so they could sneak out without the Egyptians seeing!

GOMER
Or maybe they've just *left* already. (*Glares at HANNAH*)

BELIAL
Great. What are we going to do now?

HANNAH wanders off and starts swatting at the air.

EHUD
The only thing we can do. We try to catch up. They can't be that far ahead.

DANIEL
I don't know about that. There are hundreds of ways they could go just through the city, let alone where they might go once they're out.

SARAI
Well it's not like we're going to just sit around here waiting for the Egyptians to get over their fear and pick us up again. Do you *like* being a slave?

GOMER
Yeah, this is our one chance at freedom. We can't just give up before we even begin.

DANIEL
(*looks dubious*) All right. I suppose it's worth a try. Hannah, what on earth are you doing?

HANNAH
(*still swatting at the air*) Trying to find the invisible people.

SARAI
(*goes to HANNAH and leads her gently back to the group*) Hannah, they're not invisible. They're gone.

HANNAH
Oh. Right. I knew that.

IN SEARCH OF FREEDOM

EHUD
(*sitting off from the rest of the group*) Gomer, come and look at this map with me.

GOMER joins EHUD. The rest stand around in silence for a second.

DANIEL
I can't believe you didn't hear the trumpets. How can you not hear trumpets?

HANNAH
Well so-rry. I can't help it if I'm a heavy sleeper.

BELIAL
Heaver sleeper? The whole *town* was awake! How can you sleep through that?

HANNAH
Well it's hardly just my fault. I'm not the only one left behind here, am I?

DANIEL
Yes, but we're only here because we were waiting for you!

HANNAH
Are you saying this is all my fault?

BELIAL
(*pretends to think for a second*) Uh, yes. Yes, I think we are.

SARAI
Oh boys, be nice!

GOMER
Knock it off guys. There's no point arguing now. We need to figure out which way to go.

EHUD
So. Gomer and I have been looking at this map, and we reckon that Israelites would have gone this way. (*Turns map up the other way*) I mean this way.

HANNAH
Left? I think they would have gone left. Left is a good direction.

GOMER
Hannah, for once in your life try to be sensible. We're not going left, that's where the sewerage works are. We're going to go this way.

BELIAL
Who died and made you in charge?

GOMER
Why does someone need to have died for me to be in charge?

BELIAL
Well it's not like we would vote you in!

GOMER
I don't care! You think I'm going to let one of you be in charge? Hannah can't even get *herself* anywhere on time, let alone lead a group. Daniel would take half an hour to make one simple decision, and you would just ignore everyone and do whatever you wanted!

DANIEL
Which is clearly *so* different from what you're doing.

BELIAL
(*sarcastic*) Wait, you're forgetting. She consulted Ehud. So she's not ignoring *all* of us.

DANIEL
Oh yeah. Clearly.

DANIEL and BELIAL continue mocking GOMER in the background.

SARAI and EHUD notice HEPZIBAH sitting to one side, motionless.

SARAI
Hey, what do you think she's doing?

EHUD
Dunno. Maybe she knows which way the Israelites went though. Let's go see.

GOMER
(*sees EHUD and SARAI leave*) What's happening? Oh! An Israelite! Let's ask her for directions!

EHUD
(*mutters*) That's what we were *going* to do.

HANNAH
(*spots HEPZIBAH*) Wow. *She's* hardly a picture, is she.

SARAI
Hannah! Don't be so nasty! Look at her clothes. She's an Israelite, too. She probably knows which way we should go.

HANNAH
But I *know* which way to go! We have to go left!

SARAI
(*rolls her eyes*) Come on.

By now the others are over near HEPZIBAH, who is sitting cross-legged with her eyes closed. BELIAL waves a hand in front of her face. When she doesn't react, DANIEL nudges her gently with a toe.

GOMER
(*to DANIEL*) Stop that! Uh, excuse me, Ma'am?

HEPZIBAH ignores them.

GOMER
Uh, Ma'am? (*beat*) Ma'am?

HEPZIBAH
(*heaves an exaggerated sigh, clearly irritated at being disturbed.*) Yes? What is it?

GOMER
Uh, we were wondering if you could tell us which way the Israelites went?

HEPZIBAH
(*closes her eyes and points in opposite directions*) That way.

HANNAH
Oh, well, *that's* a big help.

DANIEL
This woman's even more cracked than Hannah.

BELIAL
And that's saying something.

HANNAH
Hey!

GOMER

Ma'am, could you be a little more specific at all? It's kind of important...

HEPZIBAH sits silently.

DANIEL

What are you doing, anyway?

BELIAL

Yeah, how come you're not following the Israelites?

HEPZIBAH

I am not following the Israelites, because if God had intended me to be free, I would have been born without chains. (*Holds up her wrists, exposing previously unseen chains*)

HANNAH

(*confused*) But, you were born without chains. How could a woman give birth to chains? I mean, I saw little Isaac last week, only a few hours after he'd been born, and he didn't have chains...

HEPZIBAH

(*to GOMER*) Is she serious?

GOMER

Unfortunately, yes.

HEPZIBAH

I meant metaphorical chains, child. Though these are real enough. If God wanted me to be a free woman, then I'd have been born a free woman, yes?

SARAI

I'm not so sure about that. Aren't we supposed to believe that God has the power to change things?

HEPZIBAH

Yes, yes, that's all well and good. But do you see God in this? Have you seen any angels of the Lord recently, marching around the streets commanding Pharaoh to let God's people go?

EHUD

Ah, actually...

HEPZIBAH
Don't even *think* of saying Moses. Young scamp! So an Egyptian prince grew a conscience and decided to stand up to his people. Well he should. But what's God got to do with that? Moses is just an arrogant little *Egyptian*. (*beat*) If God wants me to be free, then He'll come and tell me so Himself. If there's one thing God's not, it's lazy.

DANIEL
Well, that's true.

GOMER
What on earth are you talking about? You can't possibly agree with her!

DANIEL
I was just agreeing that God isn't lazy!

BELIAL
Though she makes a good point about Moses. I've always thought there was something up with him. That weird stutter, for a start. And who is he, after all? A spoiled prince with a guilt complex, just like she says. Not exactly an upstanding citizen.

SARAI
What? Don't be ridiculous! Do you have eyes? You saw the miracles he performed.

BELIAL
(*shrugs*) I don't know about that. All I know is he's one shifty fellow. I mean, where was he really all those years?

SARAI
But he's rescuing us from the Egyptians!

BELIAL
Ah, that's what he says. How do you know he is, though? Might still be in league with them, for all we know.

SARAI
I *don't* know. But I trust him. And more than that, I trust that God is leading him.

BELIAL
Well, good for you. (*Suddenly decisive*) Personally, I trust that God is leading me.

EHUD
What are you saying?

BELIAL
I think I'm going to go this way. See you in the Promised Land. Or not. (*Waves and goes to exit*)

SARAI
Belial! Belial, wait! What about sticking with the group? What about loyalty? Do you really think you can make it better on your own?

BELIAL
Uh, have you looked at this group?

DANIEL
Come on, Belial, they're not *that* bad.

EHUD
Two are better than one. If one falls down, his friend can help him up. But if someone falls alone... He's stuffed.

BELIAL
Whatever. I'm going. See you later.

BELIAL exits.

HANNAH
(*tunes back in to the conversation*) What was all that about?

DANIEL
Belial's decided he wants to find his own way to the Promised Land. He left.

HANNAH
Oh. Cool. He went left?

DANIEL
Uh, no. He went that way.

HANNAH
Oh ok. I'll stay with you guys then.

DANIEL
Yippee.

GOMER
So, anyone *else* want to leave? Anyone else thinks they're good enough to make it on their own?

The others lower their gaze and shuffled awkwardly, but shake their heads.

GOMER

Good. Let's go then.

ACT II

Scene 1

In the street, in front of an Egyptian house.

Two Egyptian women, NEFERTARI and JAMILA, recline on chairs, center stage. JAMILA's hair is a mess.

NEFERTARI

Lovely day.

JAMILA

Yes, it's so good to have warm weather again. Can you believe it was only thirty degrees last week? (*Shivers at the memory*)

NEFERTARI

I know, it was awful, wasn't it. Hot today though. Would you like a drink?

JAMILA

A drink would be great, thanks.

NEFERTARI

(*nods*) Slave! Slave! Drinks!

JAMILA

Still, I hope it doesn't get too hot this summer. Remember two summers ago when it was extra hot, and all our make-up melted? That was dreadful.

NEFERTARI

SLAVE! Why doesn't that disobedient slave come?

JAMILA

Uh, we don't have slaves any more. They left.

NEFERTARI

Oh. Yes. (*Beat*) I just can't get used to it, you know. I had to make my own breakfast this morning.

JAMILA
(*horrified*) No!

NEFERTARI
Yes. I broke a nail, too. (*Holds up nail for JAMILA's inspection*)

JAMILA
That's simply awful! I mean, I knew my family had it bad, but we only lost one slave. You must have lost...

NEFERTARI
(*nods*) Ten. Yes. Disastrous.

JAMILA
(*shakes her head*) Simply dreadful. I had style my own wig this morning, you know. (*Beat*) I think I missed something.

NEFERTARI
(*aside*) You think?

JAMILA
It's going to be dreadful. Think of all the things we're going to have to do ourselves, now that the Israelites have gone. (*Counts on fingers*) Bathe, fix our hair, get dressed...

NEFERTARI
Prepare our food, go shopping... (*Gasps*) Clean the house!

Enter GOMER, EHUD, DANIEL, HANNAH and SARAI.

JAMILA
Hey look! Israelites! Maybe they decided to stay. We could make them be our slaves.

The ISRAELITES notice the two EGYPTIANS.

DANIEL
Look, there are some Egyptian girls over there.

GOMER
Daniel, I hardly think this is the time or place...

DANIEL
I was going to ask them for directions.

GOMER
Oh, right.

The ISRAELITES approach NEFERTARI and JAMILA, nudging each other and having a whispered argument about who will speak. The ISRAELITES push a reluctant EHUD forward.

EHUD
Uh, hello?

NEFERTARI
(*looks him up and down*) Hello.

EHUD
We were just wondering... Have you seen any Israelites lately?

NEFERTARI
Actually, we've seen a distinct *lack* of them lately. Disobedient slaves.

JAMILA
(*eyeing the girls*) None of you know how to do hair, do you?

HANNAH
(*from the back of the group*) Ooo, oo, I do!

SARAI
Hannah, shush!

EHUD
Ah, no. We're just trying to figure out which way the Israelites went. Do you know, at all?

JAMILA
Well, I heard old Seti complaining that they'd trampled his precious garden when I walked here this morning.

DANIEL
(*looks pleased*) Great! And which way is Seti's garden?

JAMILA
(*points right*) That way, about four streets over.

NEFERTARI
(*suspicious*) Why do you want to know which way the Israelites went?

GOMER
Uh, we're Israelites.

NEFERTARI
You're not trying to join them are you?

EHUD
Why else would we want to know where they went?

NEFERTARI
Well in that case, they went that way.

JAMILA
(*to NEFERTARI*) What? Seti's house is that way!

NEFERTARI
Shh! We don't *want* them to leave! Do you want to have to do your hair every day?

JAMILA
Ooohhh. Right. (*To ISRAELITES*) Yep, definitely that way.

EHUD
(*slightly suspicious*) Thanks. (*Returns to other ISRAELITES*) Come on, guys. They said to go this way.

The ISRAELITES walk off LEFT.

HANNAH
Hey, we're finally going left! I *told* you we had to go left.

GOMER
(*annoyed*) Ehud, are you *sure* they said to go left? I thought that girl pointed right to begin with.

EHUD
(*muttering*) I know, but they both said left in the end. What can we do? We have to try something.

The ISRAELITES continue walking. The EGYPTIANS exit surreptitiously.

The ISRAELITES walk back and forth on the stage a couple of times.

EHUD
Ok, this is the forth street.

IN SEARCH OF FREEDOM

The ISRAELITES look around.

GOMER
I don't think they would have come through here. These streets are really narrow.

HANNAH
But we went left! So we must be on the right track!

EHUD
I think we need to find someone else to ask.

DANIEL
There's a girl over there. (*Points to HATHOR standing down stage right.*) She might know.

The ISRAELITES approach HATHOR.

EHUD
Excuse me, do you know which way the Israelites went?

HATHOR
Why do you want to know?

EHUD
Does it matter?

HATHOR
Yes, actually, it does.

DANIEL
Why should we tell you our plans? You might be trying to trick us, or something...

SARAI
Oh Daniel, don't be silly. She's only one young girl. (To *HATHOR*) We got... accidentally left behind. We're trying to catch up.

HATHOR
All right. I know which way they went. But I'll only tell you on one condition.

The ISRAELITES look nervously at one another.

DANIEL
What's that?

HATHOR
I want to come too.

SARAI

What? Why?

HATHOR

I want freedom.

HANNAH

But you *are* free. You're not a slave.

HATHOR

Have you ever been treated nicely by an Egyptian? Any of you?

The ISRAELITES shuffle, trying to avoid answering.

HATHOR

Well? Have you?

GOMER

(*glances around the group and answers quietly for all of them*) No.

HATHOR

Well there you go.

HANNAH

I still don't understand. (*To SARAI*) Is it just me?

SARAI

No, I don't understand either.

HATHOR

You want to be free from being slaves. I want to be free from being a slaver.

HANNAH

I still don't get it.

HATHOR

We've had slaves almost as long as I can remember. Nubians, Canaanites, Syrians, and of course Israelites. The Israelites always stood out to me. Do you know why?

The ISRAELITES shake heads in the negative.

HATHOR
Because the Israelites always had hope. Even though they were enslaved, there was something about them—about you—that fascinated me. And eventually, I figured it out. You may be slaves, but because of your hope in God, you're freer than most Egyptians I know. And I want that kind of freedom. I want to worship your God.

EHUD
Are you sure?

HATHOR
Yes, I'm sure.

GOMER
But what about everything you'd leave behind?

HATHOR
(*shrugs*) Isn't freedom worth any price? (*Beat*) So, how 'bout it? Am I in?

SARAI
Of course! (*She hugs HATHOR*) Welcome.

GOMER
Not to be practical or anything, but can you tell us which way they went now? We're kind of in a hurry.

HATHOR
Sure. Right this way.

They exit, chatting happily.

ACT III

Scene 1

The FIVE ISRAELITES and HATHOR enter.

HANNAH
I still think we should have turned left coming out of the town.

DANIEL
You *always* want to go left!

HANNAH
Because that's the way we should have gone!

DANIEL
You can't always go left, we explained that to you yesterday!

HANNAH
(*pouts*) But I *like* going left.

GOMER
Oh for crying out loud, Hannah. Will you stop going on about that idiotic 'left' thing! If you always go left you'll go in a circle, are you really too stupid to understand that?

DANIEL
Hey, don't call her stupid!

GOMER
Why not?! She is!

HANNAH
I am *not* stupid! You're stupid!

DANIEL
(*to GOMER*) Yeah, you think you're so good, so smart, but where has *your* leadership got us? Can you see the Israelites anywhere? Hannah, can you see them?

HANNAH
No. But maybe that's just 'cause I'm *stupid*. (*Glares at GOMER*)

GOMER
(*To DANIEL*) You were just as frustrated with her a second ago! Why are you siding with her now? That's right, it's everyone against me…

SARAI
(*notices something happening behind the audience*) Uh, guys?

GOMER
I'm just so stupid, aren't I. So horrible, and awful, and mean!

SARAI
Guys?

GOMER
I'd like to see any of *you* navigate your way through town!

IN SEARCH OF FREEDOM

DANIEL
I can navigate perfectly well, thank you.

SARAI
Hello? People!

HANNAH
Yeah, it's easy! You just turn left!

GOMER
Gar!! You're pathetic! The Israelites are just lucky *you're* not leading them—they'd be wandering the desert for YEARS!

SARAI
(*shouting*) GUYS!!! Look! (*Points out over audience*)

The ISRAELITES and HATHOR turn to look out over the audience and their jaws drop.

EHUD
Whoa.

There is silence for a while as they absorb the scene.

HANNAH
The water! That's amazing!

GOMER
It's like... It's like something's parting the sea!

HATHOR
Some*one*, you mean.

DANIEL
Hey, what's that down there, in the dry bit between the water?

GOMER
It looks like people. It is! Look! There's a chariot! It's the Egyptian army!

HANNAH
Hellooo! Little people! Oh, hey, I know that guy! Hey, whipman, over here! (*Waves frantically*)

GOMER
(*elbows HANNAH in the ribs*) Stop that! Do you *want* him to come over here? Really? You *like* being whipped? 'Cause that's what he'll do if he sees us. And then he'll drag us back to town by our hair, and leave us to starve in prison for a week!

HANNAH
Oh. Yeah. I knew that. (*Quietly*) Never mind, Mr Whipman. You just keep charioting along.

FX: Wind and wave noises, continuing until indicated below.

DANIEL
Look, the water's starting to come down on that side!

EHUD
Yeah, look, they're getting wet feet.

SARAI
(*with distaste*) More than wet feet. They're drowning. Oh look, those poor horses!

DANIEL
Ha! Take that you smelly Egyptian army. Think you're so tough, beating us up. *Now* who's laughing. (*Laughs fakely*)

SARAI
Daniel! (*Indicates HATHOR, then moves to put her arm around her*)

GOMER
(*looks HATHOR up and down appraisingly*) Well, it was her choice after all. I think we're entitled to feel a little joyous, Sarai. They didn't exactly treat us like royalty.

FX: During SARAI's line the wind and wave noises cease.

SARAI
I know that. I have just as many scars from beatings as you do. But they're still people, and they're still dying. And good or bad, they were Hathor's people. You could show a little respect.

EHUD
(*nods towards the 'sea'*) Well, it's over now, anyway. They're all gone. I hope our lot made it through.

Beat.

IN SEARCH OF FREEDOM

GOMER

Smooth as glass. You'd never guess it was split a few minutes ago.

SARAI

Or that a few thousand people just drowned there.

HANNAH

I hope they made it.

Another beat, slightly awkward.

EHUD

Hey! (*Points to a figure sitting front stage right*) Look everyone! Look, it's Belial!

The ISRAELITES rush over to BELIAL and surround him with hugs and pats on the back. HATHOR follows uncertainly.

HANNAH

Hey, Belial! Did you get lost too? We didn't go left, that's why we got lost...

GOMER

(*glares at HANNAH*) We're NOT lost!

DANIEL

So, Belial, how'd you end up here? What happened?

GOMER

(*spiteful*) Yeah. Couldn't make it on your own?

BELIAL

I'm doing just fine on my own thank you.

GOMER

Sure you are—

SARAI

Gomer, just be quiet will you?

GOMER sulks.

DANIEL

(*to BELIAL*) So, seriously, what have you been doing?

ALL sit to hear his story.

BELIAL
(*shrugs*) Not much to tell, really. I asked for directions, and made my way out of town. Just as I was coming up over that hill I heard this huge thundering noise. I turned back and got the fright of my life—Pharaoh's army was coming after me!

GOMER
Pssh. How could you think they were coming after *you*? As if Pharaoh would send his whole army just to get you.

SARAI
Shh!

BELIAL
I hid in those rocks back there, and when the army went thundering past I figured that they were probably actually after the main Israelite group. (*Glares at GOMER*) So I waited till they'd gone past, then I snuck out behind them. I watched them go into the sea after the Israelites, and I saw the sea crash down on them. (*Shrugs*) That's all, really.

Beat.

EHUD
What's that?

DANIEL
What's what?

EHUD
That.

ALL squint into the distance, over the audience's heads.

SARAI
That looks like people on the ridge!

BELIAL
Couldn't be. No one could have survived that.

GOMER
No, look, it is people! The Israelites, they made it!

SARAI
They're ok!

GOMER
This is great! All we have to do is find our way around the edge of the sea, and we can follow them into the desert!

DANIEL
Follow them into the desert? I don't know...

BELIAL
(*sarcastic*) Oh, come on Daniel. That sounds like a great idea. I'd love to die in the desert. (*Turns to GOMER*) Weren't enough graves in Egypt, were there? Wanted to bring us out here where there was more space to bury us all, did you? (*Walks away in disgust. Begins pacing out a rectangle on the far side of the stage.*)

EHUD
Gomer, they do have a point. The Israelites will be long gone by the time we make it around.

HANNAH
And the sea is *huge*! I don't want to walk all the way around it! It's all... dirty!

GOMER
Ehud, I think we can make it. God is with us. He convinced Pharaoh to let us go. In comparison, catching up with the Israelites is nothing.

EHUD
Okay. I agree; we can't do it, but God can. If he truly wants us to be free, well, then... (*Shrugs*) We'll make it somehow.

HANNAH
(*notices BELIAL pacing*) Belial, what are you doing?

BELIAL
(*still pacing*) Hmm?

HANNAH
What are you doing?

BELIAL
Measuring out my grave. Anyone have a shovel?

SARAI
Oh ha ha ha. Very funny.

BELIAL
Well, you might be content to die, following that freak (*nods at Gomer*) into the desert, but I for one am rather attached to my life.

GOMER
Life? What life? We're *slaves*, Belial, *slaves*. We have no lives.

EHUD
Think about it Belial. Real freedom, at last.

BELIAL
(*stops pacing and confronts the group*) I am thinking about it. You think I'm not? You don't think I know what I'm missing out on because *she* (*points at Hannah*) slept in?

HANNAH
(*aside*) It's not *my* fault we didn't go left.

BELIAL
Think about it, you say. Well I am. And I think I'd rather be a slave for the Egyptians than die in the desert.

SARAI
Belial, no, you don't mean that!

DANIEL
(*quietly*) I think he does, Sarai. And actually, I think I do too. I'm sorry Ehud, Gomer. I just don't believe that you'll catch up to them. Until now, I thought we had a chance. But after this... (*Gestures out over the 'sea'*) It could take weeks to go around, and they'll be long gone by then. And once we get out into the open desert... We've no food, no water... I just... I'd just rather be alive.

SARAI
(*almost in tears*) No, you can't mean it.

EHUD
(*looks to HANNAH and HATHOR for their opinion*) Well?

HATHOR
(*shrugs*) I didn't run away from home for nothing. I know where I'm going.

EHUD
Hannah?

IN SEARCH OF FREEDOM

HANNAH
(*flustered, indecisive*) I don't know! I mean, we've come all this way... But I don't want to walk all the way around the sea... I mean, that's a lot more work than doing Egyptian hair... Maybe those girls we met yesterday would take me on. I *like* hair and make-up... I don't like walking. (*Beat*) I think I'll go back too. I'm sorry.

EHUD
Well, all right then. Good luck.

EHUD shakes hands with BELIAL and DANIEL. He pauses before HANNAH, who throws her arms around him and sobs theatrically. EHUD is startled and unsure how to respond.

SARAI and GOMER hug the boys, then pry HANNAH away from EHUD to hug her also.

Now that the final moment has come, BELIAL is a bit shy.

BELIAL
Well, bye then.

DANIEL
Good luck.

HANNAH
(*distressed*) I'm sorry. I really am.

GOMER
It's ok Hannah.

BELIAL, DANIEL and HANNAH turn to leave.

GOMER
Hannah?

HANNAH
(*turns back*) Yes?

GOMER
I... I don't think you're stupid.

HANNAH
(*stares for a second, then wipes her eyes*) Thanks Gomer. Thanks.

BELIAL, DANIEL and HANNAH exit.

SARAI collapses to the ground and cries.

GOMER
(*goes to SARAI and gives her a hug*) Aw, Sarai, don't cry.

SARAI
But how can they just go back like that? How can they give up so easily?

EHUD
(*shrugs*) Freedom's a hard thing. Some people just aren't ready for it.

GOMER
You can't make their decision for them, Sarai. You just have to make yours, and stick to it.

SARAI
But it's just not fair! They don't know what they're missing.

HATHOR
But you can't tell them.

SARAI
(*looks to HATHOR in surprise; she didn't expect her to speak*) What?

HATHOR
You can't tell them, Sarai. Take it from me, people either get it, or they don't. My family... Well, they're freer than your people were, in a way. But in another way... Freedom is what you make it, and real freedom, true freedom... You can't explain it. You can only understand it. It's a decision that you either make, or you don't.

SARAI
(*wipes her eyes*) You know, I think I know what you mean. (*Beat*) I still wish they could have understood.

HATHOR
I know.

EHUD, who had been hanging back, now intrudes.

EHUD
Girls, I think it's time.

EHUD crouches between GOMER and SARAI

EHUD
Are you ready?

SARAI

(*takes a deep breath*) I'm ready.

GOMER

Me too. I've waited my whole life for this.

EHUD

Hathor?

HATHOR

(*grins*) I thought you'd never ask.

EHUD links arms with GOMER and with SARAI, who links arms with HATHOR. EHUD pulls them to a standing position.

EHUD

A journey of a thousand miles starts with just one step. And this, ladies, is our first step on the road to freedom.

SARAI

(*nods*) Let's go.

Exit all.

THE JOURNEY

Moses rallies the Israelites after the crossing of the Red Sea. After the Israelites camp on the far shore for a month or so, Sarai reunites with her family and Moses and Miriam sing thanks to God in preparation for moving off into the desert.

Partway into the journey, the people begin to grow hungry. Sarai is still amazed by her freedom and glad that she was able to catch up, but her sister Abigail grows weary. Quails appear for dinner, manna arrives for breakfast, and Moses speaks to the people to address the complaints that are occurring.

Moses leaves the camp to climb Mount Horeb. Upon his return he discovers that the camp have reverted to idolatry. Furious, he breaks the golden calf, melting it down and feeding it to the people through the water supply. On behalf of his people, Moses begs God for forgiveness.

Forty years later, Joshua finally makes preparations to lead the people of Israel into the promised land. Representatives from each tribe come forward and together they celebrate the new life God has given them.

ACTORS REQUIRED:

Male: 5

Female: 5

Either: 0

MINIMUM TOTAL: 9

THE JOURNEY

SCENE SYNOPSIS

Act 1

SCENE 1
Moses despairs about the Israelites' complaining and informs them that the real journey is only just about to begin.

SCENE 2
Sarai is reunited with her family. Moses gives praise to God with the people.

Act 2

SCENE 1
The people complain that they are hungry and Moses tells them there will be meat for dinner and bread for breakfast.

SCENE 2
Quails arrive for dinner.

SCENE 3
Aaron finds manna on the ground in the morning, and Moses gives thanks.

SCENE 4
Moses announces that God is going to come and speak to the people from the mountain to show that He is guiding Moses.

SCENE 5
The people are terrified of God and beg Moses to speak to Him for them. Moses tells them that God has commanded them not to worship any other gods, and leaves to go up the mountain.

SCENE 6
After a month of waiting, the people go to Aaron and convince him to give them something to follow.

Act 3

SCENE 1

Moses and Joshua return to the people and are horrified to find them worshipping a golden calf.

SCENE 2

Moses separates out those have obeyed God and those who have disobeyed. Those who disobeyed he makes drink water with the ground down calf to accept the weight of their sins.

SCENE 3

Moses begs God for forgiveness on behalf of the people, and God agrees for Moses' sake.

Act 4

SCENE 1

Moses informs Joshua that he is to be the next leader of the Israalites.

SCENE 2

Moses announces Joshua as leader to the Israelites.

Act 5

SCENE 1

Joshua prepares to lead the Israelites finally into the Promised Land.

THE JOURNEY

CAST OF CHARACTERS

MIRIAM
Moses' sister. Quiet and thoughtful. Has a good feel for the emotional temperature of the people.

MOSES
God's chosen leader. Still not certain why God chose him. Feels the weight of his responsibility.

TAMAR
Israelite. Mother of Abigail and Sarai.

ABIGAIL
Israelite teen. Daughter of Tamar, younger sister of Sarai. Somewhat impatient.

SARAI
Israelite teen. Daughter of Tamar, older sister of Abigail. Patient, kind.

MAN
An Israelite man. A complainer.

WOMAN
An Israelite woman. A complainer.

AARON
Moses' brother. Impulsive and rash. Gets carried away easily.

ISRAELITES
All Israelites collectively, usually including Man, Woman, Sarai and Abigail.

JOSHUA
Moses' right-hand man. A righteous, godly man.

LORD
The Lord God. May be performed as a voice-over.

THE JOURNEY

ACT I

Scene 1

Evening. Shores of the Red Sea. MOSES stands alone, separate from the rest of the ISRAELITES (including TAMAR, ABIGAIL, MIRIAM and AARON), who are hugging and reassuring one another and generally talking. MOSES is exhausted, mentally, emotionally, and physically.

MIRIAM notices MOSES standing alone and after a bit excuses herself from the conversation.

MIRIAM

Are you okay?

MOSES

(*Tired, trying to keep a brave face*) Yes. Yes, I'm fine. (*He stares out towards the Sea*) Do you wonder about the people, Miriam? The soldiers? I... knew some of them.

MIRIAM

Oh, Moses. (*hugs*) I'm sorry.

MOSES

(*softly*) The Lord's will be done. Pharaoh hardened his heart. I asked him to listen. I begged him!

MIRIAM

Moses, it isn't your fault. The Egyptians? They weren't your responsibility. The people, though... (*indicates the ISRAELITES*). You must come and say something to them, Moses. They need to hear the word of the Lord.

MOSES

He held back the waters so they could cross on dry land. The entire Egyptian army has perished. What more could they want?

MIRIAM

(*gently*) You. A person. Something to remind them in the face of God's terrifying power that He still loves them.

MOSES
(*beat, then sigh*) You're right. Go and gather them.

MIRIAM gathers the ISRAELITES around. MOSES takes a moment to compose himself, then goes out to meet the ISRAELITES.

MOSES
Israelites. Today, you have seen God move in very powerful ways. After leading us for a month through the deserts, He has finally allowed us to cross the Red Sea—and in spectacular fashion. When was the last time any of you saw God work as you have seen Him work today? When have you sensed His power so near, so raw, so strong?

And yet, many of you may be tempted to think that this is the end of the journey. God has kept us safe this far, and now we are here together.

Let me be clear: this is this beginning. Our month of wandering was just a prelude to the real trek we face now as we strike out across deserts more vast than any we have yet seen. But don't worry about the future. The problems we will face in the desert are problems we cannot even possibly image right now, problems we may not even have names for—but God knows them. God knows our futures, each and every one of us, and He knows how to keep us safe.

As we journey across the deserts now, be strong. Be faithful. Have courage. Our God is with us.

The Pillar of Fire appears. ISRAELITES are amazed.

MOSES retreats once more, and MIRIAM follows.

MIRIAM
That was very well done.

MOSES
(*still tired*) Praise God. Let's just go make camp.

Scene 2

Late evening in the Israelite camp. Fires are lit and families are finishing their evening meal. ABIGAIL and sits outside her tent.

Enter TAMAR.

TAMAR
Are you alright?

THE JOURNEY

ABIGAIL

What? Oh, yes. Yes, I'm okay. (*beat*) I just... Every time I close my eyes, I see the water.

TAMAR

I do too.

ABIGAIL

Towering up, so high I thought it would drown the sky. How did it stay up, Mum? How?

TAMAR

Oh sweetheart. Our God is a powerful God, and that can be really scary sometimes.

ABIGAIL

(*nods*) All those soldiers. All those horses. (*shudder*) The sound. I can't... I hear them when I try to sleep.

They hug. After a pause, a rustle is heard offstage.

SARAI, clothes dirty and ragged and hardly recognisable, enters. She walks towards ABIGAIL and TAMAR.

TAMAR sees SARAI and freezes. Could this really be her missing daughter?

ABIGAIL

Sarai? Sarai, is that you?

ABIGAIL and TAMAR scramble to their feet. There are relieved hugs all round.

TAMAR

But how? When we left Egypt without you, I thought I'd never see you again!

ABIGAIL

You're alive!

SARAI

So are you!

TAMAR

But how did you find us?

SARAI

(*points to the Pillar of Fire*)

ABIGAIL

Oh.

SARAI
It's kind of obvious. We followed it all the way out from Egypt.

TAMAR
We?

SARAI
Daniel, Ehud, Gomer and I. They've found their families already.

Trumpets sound.

TAMAR hustles the girls side stage.

SARAI
What's happening?

TAMAR
It's Moses, he's coming out to speak.

SARAI
Moses! Really?

ABIGAIL
Oh, he speaks to us all the time. It's no big deal.

SARAI
But it's *Moses*! The man who conquered Pharaoh! The man God used to send the plagues! Moses!

TAMAR
Hush now.

AARON and MIRIAM enter ahead of MOSES.

SARAI
What will he say?

TAMAR
Hush!

MOSES
People of Israel! Our Lord has delivered us!

SARAI, TAMAR and ABIGAIL cheer as with a crowd.

THE JOURNEY

MOSES

Oh Lord! Who among gods is like you? Who is like you, majestic in holiness, awesome in glory, working wonders? In your unfailing love you will lead the people you have redeemed. In your strength you will guide them to your holy dwelling. The nations will hear and tremble.

MOSES and MIRIAM sing.*

MOSES AND MIRIAM

Sing to the Lord,
Exalt His name.
The horse and its rider
He has thrown into the sea.
The Lord is my strength
And my song.
He has become
My salvation.

He is my God
I will praise Him
Heav'nly Father
I'll exalt Him
Pharaoh's chariots
And his army
Hurled into the sea.

He is my God
I will praise Him
Heav'nly Father
I'll exalt Him
Pharaoh's chariots
And his army
Hurled into the sea.

God reigns eternally.
He set His people free.

* See www.amylaurens.com/books/where-your-treasure-is/ for suggested music.

THE JOURNEY

ACT II

Scene 1

Israelite camp. Morning, several days later. SARAI and ABIGAIL are wandering through the camp.

ABIGAIL

I'm hungry.

SARAI

Me too.

ABIGAIL

Why didn't Moses think about this when he told us all to pack up and leave? We have the whole desert to cross, and we're not going to get anywhere if we all die of starvation first.

SARAI

(*sigh*) Abigail, you know it's not that simple. And if you ask him like that all you're likely to get is yelled at.

ABIGAIL pulls a face but they keep walking, eventually arriving at the Meeting Place where MOSES and AARON are being harassed by a crowd of people. The people are in a line, waiting to see MOSES and AARON, who talk quietly with the people at the head of the line. Farther along, people start to shout out.

MAN

Why did you bring us out here to die? I'd rather a quick death at the hands of the Egyptians than slow starvation!

WOMAN

In Egypt we had pots of meat, all-you-can-eat every night!

MAN

You've brought us here to starve!

WOMAN

I'm hungry! My children are hungry! Feed us!

ABIGAIL

I'm hungry too!

SARAI elbows her.

THE JOURNEY

MOSES
Enough!

AARON
Stop your complaints, and your pestering! Who are we, that you should grumble at us?

MAN
You brought us here!

WOMAN
Yeah, you brought us!

MOSES
Stop! Stop, calm down. The Lord has heard your whining, and in the evening, you will know that it was He who brought you out of Egypt.

The crowd whispers.

ABIGAIL
What do you suppose *that* means?

SARAI
I don't know, just be quiet and listen!

MOSES
(*raises his hands for quiet*) At twilight, you will have meat, and in the morning, bread. Then you will know the power of the Lord.

AARON
At twilight, come before the Lord, and he will feed you. But for now, if you're here to complain about being hungry, go away!

The crowd begins to disperse.

ABIGAIL
Well. How do you think they're going to manage *that*? I don't care if he *is* Moses. Where can he possibly find enough meat to fill the entire Israelite camp?

SARAI
(*quietly, watching MOSES*) I don't know, Abigail. I... Come on. Let's go tell Mum.

ABIGAIL and SARAI exit.

Scene 2

Twilight. ABIGAIL is hurriedly adjusting her clothing.

Enter SARAI.

SARAI
Abigail, hurry up! I told Mum to take Jared and go. Why aren't you ready?

ABIGAIL
I nearly am! There, all set. Now we can go.

SARAI and ABIGAIL hurry through the streets.

ABIGAIL
I should have worn my cloak. It's colder than I thought.

SARAI
Well, that's what happens in the desert. It gets cold at night.

A flapping noise begins, increasing as the girls talk.

ABIGAIL
Well how am I supposed to know what a stupid desert is like? A month ago I lived in a house in this fantastic place called Egypt. You might have heard of it?

SARAI
Hilarious, Abigail. You were also a slave and had to live at your mistress's beck and call.

ABIGAIL
So? At least I was warm.

SARAI
(*stops*) What's that noise?

ABIGAIL
What noise?

Flapping grows louder.

SARAI
THAT noise.

SARAI and ABIGAIL peer around.

THE JOURNEY

SARAI

Oh! Abi! Look!

ABIGAIL

What in the world...?

SARAI

Birds! (*laughs*) Meat! He promised us meat!

ABIGAIL

(*nervous*) Sarai, the birds... they're heading right towards us. You don't think... we should hide?

SARAI

(*too busy being excited about Moses' prediction coming true to care about her sister's anxiety*) Birds!!

The flock of quail floods the street in front of them. ABIGAIL shrieks and ducks, covering her head, but SARAI throws out her arms and laughs as the birds fly all around her.

Scene 3

MOSES, in his tent. Enter AARON.

AARON

Moses! Moses, you must come and see this!

MOSES

What?

AARON

The ground! It's... I'm not even sure what it is. Please, come see!

MOSES and AARON exit the tent. Outside, they stare in wonder at the ground.

MOSES

It's white.

AARON

Yes, I can see that. But what is it?

MOSES crouches to examine the substance, running his finger through it and sniffing it. He smile.

MOSES

Aaron, it's food!

AARON
Food?

MOSES
Bread. He said He would provide bread. (*tastes it*) Tastes like honey wafers.

AARON
(*tastes*) Amazing. But what *is* it?

MOSES
No idea. It's... It's Whatever It Is.

Enter MIRIAM.

MIRIAM
What are you doing? Why are you eating dirt?

AARON
It isn't dirt, it's (*exchanges glances with MOSES*) WhateverItIs.

MIRIAM
(*raises eyebrow*) I'm sure it is.

MOSES
No really, try some.

MIRIAM tries some.

MIRIAM
Well, praise the Lord. He really did send us bread.

MOSES
Of course He did. Go and rouse the people. Tell them to collect whatever they need. An omer. (*To AARON*) Three and two-thirds of a litre per person should be enough, shouldn't it?

AARON
How should I know?

MIRIAM
Psh. You boys are hopeless. Yes, an omer a person will be plenty. I'll let them know.

MIRIAM goes to exit.

THE JOURNEY

MOSES
And no more! Remind them—they can't keep it til morning, so there's no point collecting more!

MIRIAM nods. Exit.

MOSES
Grab a jar, will you? Put an omer of WhateverItIs in it.

AARON
To eat?

MOSES
No. God told me to keep some. As a reminder, for the future.

AARON nods and exits.

MOSES
Thank you, Lord, for your provenance. I've no idea how you're going to get us safely across the desert, and I still have no clue why you chose me to lead your people, but... thank you. Just, thank you.

Scene 4

MOSES stands before the ISRAELITES, ready to speak. AARON, MIRIAM and JOSHUA are all with him. AARON quiets the crowd.

MOSES
Hear, O Israel. The Lord says: You have seen for yourselves what I did to Egypt, and how I carried you on eagles' wings and brought you to myself. Now if you obey me fully and keep my covenant, then out of all nations you will be my treasured possession. Although the whole earth is mine, you will be for me a kingdom of priests, and a holy nation.

ISRAELITES
We will do everything the Lord has said!

MOSES
Good. Now, in three days, the Lord is going to come and speak from a dense cloud, so that you may hear and trust that He is guiding me. You must prepare yourselves in the meantime; keep yourself pure and holy, be consecrated, and wash your clothes. In three days, we will gather together here, and the Lord will speak. Go now, and prepare.

The ISRAELITES leave, muttering amongst themselves.

MOSES

Aaron, I'm going to need your help. Joshua, you too. The Lord has said that we must set up limits around the mountain. If anyone touches the mountain, they are to die. Don't let them approach until they hear the sound of the ram's horn on the third day.

Scene 5

Three days later. MOSES and AARON and JOSHUA before the ISRAELITES.

Thunder sounds. Earthquake. The ISRAELITES fall to the ground.

ISRAELITES

Make it stop! Speak to us yourself and we will listen! Do not have God speak to us or we will die!

MOSES

Do not be afraid. God is testing you so that the fear of God will be with you and keep you from sinning.

AARON

Go, Moses! Find out what the Lord wants from us.

MOSES exits. AARON and JOSHUA help up the ISRAELITES and calm them.

MOSES enters.

MOSES

Israel! I bring another message from the Lord! Here is what He says: You have seen for yourselves that I have spoken to you from heaven. Do not make any gods to be alongside me; do not make for yourselves gods of silver or gods of gold. Make an altar of earth for me and sacrifice on it your burnt offerings and fellowship offerings, your sheep and goats and your cattle. Wherever my name is honoured, I will come to you and bless you.

ISRAELITES

We will do everything the Lord has said! We will obey!

MOSES

(*to AARON and JOSHUA*) We must go up the mountain.

AARON

We?

JOSHUA

Me too?

THE JOURNEY

                        MOSES

Yes, both of you, and the elders. You won't be able to come all the way—Aaron, you must come back down and guide the people while I am gone—but you can come to the place where God descends, where the ground is sapphire blue and the Lord will walk among us.

MOSES, JOSHUA and AARON exit.

Scene 6

AARON faces an angry crowd. MIRIAM stands to one side. ABIGAIL and SARAI are in the crowd.

There is the sense that this argument has been waging for some time, with AARON doing his best to observe and stay out of things. MIRIAM is somewhat impatient with his inaction.

                        MAN

I don't care what you think. It's been over a month! What did he expect us to do?

                        SARAI

Wait patiently!

                        ABIGAIL

Sarai, shoosh, stay out of it.

                        MAN

Wait? Wait for how long? For what? What have we heard from God since Moses left? How do we know they have not *both* abandoned us to die?

                        SARAI

Are you stupid?

                        ABIGAIL

Sarai!

                        SARAI

No, Abi, I mean it. (*to MAN*) *Are* you stupid? Can you not see the cloud over the mountain? The very prescence of God is there still, and you think He has deserted us?

                        MIRIAM

(*to AARON*) You must speak to them. You must calm them.

                        MAN

How do we know God is there? It's a cloud! We haven't heard him speak in five weeks! If God is there, he neither listens nor cares. Why then should we care?

AARON
Quiet! Quiet. (*to MAN*) What is it you want?

MIRIAM
Aaron, I don't think that—

AARON
Hush. Come now. What do you want?

MAN
If the Lord will not go before us and lead us through the desert, make us a god who can!

SARAI
No! Moses specifically said—

ABIGAIL
Oh pish. Moses? What Moses! We have no idea what's happened to him!

SARAI
No! Not you too!

MAN
(*to AARON*) What do you say? Will you give us someone we can truly follow? Will you desert us in our hour of need, just like your brother, or are you really stronger than he? Perhaps you should have led us all along.

MIRIAM
Aaron...

AARON
(*beat*) Gather the people. Collect all the gold jewelry we took from the Egyptians.

MIRIAM
Aaron!

SARAI
No!

AARON
Bring it to me. I will melt it down and give you something to follow.

MIRIAM
Aaron, you can't!

AARON
I can. If Moses will not return to lead us, then I will do it.

ACT III

Scene 1

JOSHUA waits onstage.

Enter MOSES.

JOSHUA

Moses, sir! You've returned! What does He say? What messages has the Lord given you? You've been gone so long!

MOSES

(*slightly dazed*) How long have I been away?

JOSHUA

Forty days, sir.

MOSES

Forty days! (*goes to rub his hand over his head and remembers the tablets in his hands*) Oh. Look. Inscribed by the very hand of God.

JOSHUA

What do they say?

MOSES

The laws. The laws He spoke to us all from the mountain—forty days ago.

JOSHUA is amazed.

MOSES

Come. Let us return to the camp.

MOSES and JOSHUA walk towards the camp.

Shouts are heard.

JOSHUA

Those shouts! The camp is at war!

MOSES

No. That is neither the sound of victory, nor the sound of defeat. That is signing, Joshua. Singing!

They sped up, then stare in shock and horror at the scene below.

AARON stands near a Golden Calf while the ISRAELITES dance around it. ABIGAIL is there, but SARAI and MIRIAM are not.

As the ISRAELITES and AARON see MOSES, the music and dancing cuts off.

MOSES
(*to AARON*) What did these people do to you?

AARON
Do... Do not be angry, my lord. You know yourself how prone these people are to evil!

MOSES
These people? These people! I know how prone these people are to evil! But you! I did not suspect that you were!

MOSES smashes the Calf to the ground.

MOSES
Whoever is for the Lord, rally to me!

Some ISRAELITES join him, ready to fight.

MOSES sets fire to the calf.

Scene 2

MOSES stands with AARON to his left, JOSHUA to his right. MIRIAM is behind. MOSES holds a bowl with the melted down calf.

The ISRAELITES stand in two groups in front of MOSES, one containing SARAI, one containing ABIGAIL.

MOSES
(*to the group with SARAI*) Levites! You have rallied to the Lord when he commanded. For that, you have been set apart to the Lord, and He has blessed you this day.

(*to the group with ABIGAIL*) You have committed a great sin. But now I will go up to the Lord. Perhaps I can make atonement for your sin. But first, you must accept your sin upon your shoulders.

The melted-down calf is passed out to all the ISRAELITES and they eat and/or drink.

THE JOURNEY

Scene 3

MOSES, alone.

MOSES
(*praying*) Oh, what a great sin theses people have committed! But now, please forgive their sin—and if not, then blot me out of the book that You have written!

LORD
Whoever has sinner against me, I will blot out of my book. Now go, lead the people to the place I spoke of, and my angel will go before you. However, when the time comes for me to punish, I will punish them for their sin. But leave now, go up to the land flowing with milk and honey.

MOSES
Oh Lord, you have been telling me to lead these people, but you have not said that you will come with me. You have said, "I know you by name, and you have found favour with me." If you are truly pleased with me, then teach me your ways. Remember that this nation is your people.

LORD
My presence will go with you, and I will give you rest.

MOSES
If you do not come with us, then do not make us leave. How will anyone know that we are your people unless you go with us? What else is there to distinguish us from all the other peoples of the earth?

LORD
I will do what you have asked, because I am pleased with you, and I know you by name. But now, chisel out two stone tablets like the first, and I will write on them. I will make a covenant with you: I the Lord will go with you on your journey, and I will do wonders never before done in all the world. The people you live among will see how mighty I am, if you keep my commandments throughout your journey.

ACT IV

Scene 1

MOSES and JOSHUA.

MOSES
Joshua, the Lord has told me that I will not cross the Jordan.

JOSHUA

He has? But why?

MOSES

I have not been patient with these people of God's. They have brought me to anger many times, and now I shall pay for my sins.

JOSHUA

Oh. I am sorry.

MOSES

Never mind, that's not why I have called you here. Very soon, I will talk to the people. I will tell them that I will not cross the Jordan with them. And when I do, they will want to know who shall lead them. (*beat*) The Lord has told me to commission you, for he has determined that you will cause them to inherit the land he has promised to them.

JOSHUA

Me?!

MOSES

You have seen with your own eyes that all that the Lord our God has done. He will do the same wherever you lead the people, causing the kingdoms to tremble before you. Do not be afraid of anyone; the Lord God himself will fight for you. He will never leave you or forsake you; do not be discouraged, and do not be afraid.

JOSHUA

It will be as the Lord has said.

MOSES

Go now; call the Israelites. I will speak to them.

Scene 2

MOSES stands before the people, JOSHUA at his right, AARON at his left.

MOSES

People of Israel! I am now one hundred and twenty years old, and I am no longer able to lead you. I will not cross the Jordan with you, but the Lord your God will cross over ahead of you. He will destroy the foreign nations before you. But to do this, you will need a leader – someone who stands blameless in the sight of the Lord. The Lord has commissioned Joshua to lead you across the Jordan, so be strong and courageous. Do not be afraid, for the Lord your God goes with you. He will never leave you or forsake you.

THE JOURNEY

The ISRAELITES cheer.

ACT V

Scene 1

JOSHUA stands in front of the ISRAELITES speaking.

People of Israel! Today, we are finishing our journey. We are leaving the desert! (*Crowd cheers*) Now, let one representative from each tribe come forth! Each of you is to take up a stone to serve as a sign among you. In the future, when your children see this altar and ask you what it means, tell them that the flow of the Jordan was cut off before the ark of the covenant of the Lord so that His people could cross on dry land. He did this so that all the peoples of the earth might know that the hand of the Lord is powerful. These stones are to be a memorial to you forever. Remember the Lord!

ISRAELITES

Remember the Lord!

The REPRESENTATIVES bring forth their stones and pile them before Joshua.

JOSHUA

Give thanks to God, for He has fulfilled his promises! He has been with us on our journey thus far, and He will continue to provide. We will never journey alone. Come! Let us enter the promised land!

ABOUT THE AUTHOR

High school English teacher by day, Amy is more usually found writing fantasy and science fiction for adults and young adults alike. However, over the years her reputation as a writer got her volunteered for many play-writing projects at church, and she discovered that writing plays for teens was just as much fun as writing stories for them. Being allowed to let her inner control freak out in order to direct the plays as well was just a bonus.

Find out more at http://www.amylaurens.com, or join the mailing list at http://www.amylaurens.com/mailing-list/.